COBIT® 5 – A' Man

M000232448

# Other publications by Van Haren Publishing

Van Haren Publishing (VHP) specializes in titles on Best Practices, methods and standards within four domains:
- IT and IT Management
- Architecture (Enterprise and IT)
- Business management and
- Project management

Van Haren Publishing offers a wide collection of whitepapers, templates, free e-books, trainer material etc. in the **Van Haren Publishing Knowledge Base**: www.vanharen.net for more details.

Van Haren Publishing is also publishing on behalf of leading organizations and companies: ASLBiSL Foundation, CA, Centre Henri Tudor, Gaming Works, IACCM, IAOP, IPMA-NL, ITSqc, NAF, Ngi, PMI-NL, PON, The Open Group, The SOX Institute.

Topics are (per domain):

| IT and IT Management | Architecture (Enterprise and IT) | Project Management |
|---|---|---|
| ABC of ICT | | A4-Projectmanagement |
| ASL® | Archimate® | ICB / NCB |
| CATS CM® | BIP / Novius | MINCE® |
| CMMI® | GEA® | M_o_R® |
| CoBIT | TOGAF® | MSP™ |
| Frameworx | | P3O® |
| ISO 17799 | **Business Management** | *PMBOK® Guide* |
| ISO 27001 | BiSL® | PRINCE2® |
| ISO 27002 | Contract Management | |
| ISO/IEC 20000 | EFQM | |
| ISPL | eSCM | |
| IT Service CMM | ISA-95 | |
| ITIL® | ISO 9000 | |
| MOF | ISO 9001:2000 | |
| MSF | OPBOK | |
| SABSA | SAP | |
| | SixSigma | |
| | SOX | |
| | SqEME® | |

# COBIT® 5

## A Management Guide

Pierre Bernard

# Colophon

Title:              COBIT® 5 – A Management Guide

Author:             Pierre Bernard

Editor:             Jane Chittenden

Review team:        Rob van der Burgh (Microsoft)
                    Steven de Haes (University of Antwerp)
                    Chris Jones
                    Ali Makaleh (Microsoft)
                    Hans Reh (Microsoft)
Publisher:          Van Haren Publishing, Zaltbommel, www.vanharen.net

ISBN:               978 90 8753 701 2
ISBN eBook:         978 90 8753 800 2

Print:              First Edition, first impression, October 2012

Design and Layout: CO2 Premedia BV, Amersfoort – NL

Copyright:          © Van Haren Publishing, 2012

For any further enquiries about Van Haren Publishing, please send an email to:
info@vanharen.net

# Preface

This Management Guide provides readers with two benefits. First, it is an easy accessible reference guide to IT governance for those who are not acquainted with this field. Second, it is a high-level introduction to ISACA's open standard COBIT 5.0 that will encourage further study. This guide follows the process structure of COBIT 5.0.

This guide is aimed at business and IT (service) managers, consultants, auditors and anyone interested in learning more about the possible application of IT governance standards in the IT management domain. In addition, it provides students in IT and Business Administration with a compact reference to COBIT 5.0.

Similar to the previous version of this management guide, based on COBIT 4.1, it aims at two important areas: Auditing and IT Service Management. It will offer the auditors a bridge to the service management business, and it offers the service management world a management instrument that enables them to put the pieces of the puzzle together, and get (and remain!) in control. However, compared to previous versions, COBIT 5 focuses less on auditing and revision. The influence of ITIL is strongly felt – which is not least because of service orientation – and the positioning of the service management processes within the COBIT 5 process domains can be clearly seen. Because governance and service management are ever-closer growing management disciplines, companies with IT organizations that have aligned their service management according to ITIL can enrich their management and governance with COBIT 5.

COBIT 5 has a closer alignment with ITIL than before, which confirms that IT service management and IT governance are developing in the same direction. This implies that for organizations that have organized their service management on ITIL principles, improving their IT governance based on COBIT is a logical next step.

Any comments and suggestions regarding the content of this management guide are welcomed by the COBIT 5 project team.

October 2012
The Publisher

# Table of contents

Preface .................................................................................... V
List of figures ........................................................................ XI
List of tables ........................................................................ XII

**1    Introduction and executive summary** ........................................ 1
1.1    Introduction .............................................................................. 1
1.2    What is governance of enterprise IT? .......................................... 2
       Compliance ................................................................................ 4
       What are the major focus areas that make up governance
       of enterprise IT? ........................................................................ 4
1.3    Overview of this publication ...................................................... 6
1.4    What to use? Where to start? ...................................................... 6
       What can go wrong if it's not implemented effectively? ............. 7
1.5    Implementation tips ................................................................... 8
1.6    Appendices ................................................................................. 8

**2    The COBIT 5 principles** ........................................................... 9
2.1    Principle 1: Meeting Stakeholder Needs ................................... 10
2.2    Principle 2: Covering the enterprise end-to-end ....................... 10
       Governance enablers ............................................................... 12
       Governance scope ................................................................... 12
       Roles, activities and relationships ......................................... 12
2.3    Principle 3: Applying a Single, Integrated Framework ............. 14
       Stakeholders and stakeholder needs ....................................... 14
2.4    Principle 4: Enabling a Holistic Approach ............................... 15
       Enablers .................................................................................. 16
       Systemic governance ............................................................... 16
       The generic enabler model ...................................................... 16
       The capability attribute for enablers ..................................... 18
2.5    Principle 5: Separating Governance from Management ............. 19
       Governance system .................................................................. 19
       Management .............................................................................. 19
       Interactions between governance and management ................ 20

**3      The goals cascade**..................................................................................**21**

        Introduction..................................................................................21

3.1    Using the goals cascade ............................................................. 24

        Benefits of the goals cascade ................................................... 24

        Using the goals cascade carefully.............................................. 25

        Metrics ......................................................................................... 28

3.2    Enterprise goal metrics..............................................................28

3.3    IT-related goal metrics ...............................................................28

3.4    Drivers and benefits ...................................................................31

        Drivers .........................................................................................31

        Benefits ........................................................................................31


**4      Detailed description of the enabler models** ......................... **35**

4.1    Overview of this section ............................................................35

4.2    Process model ............................................................................36

4.3    Information model ......................................................................37

        Information quality......................................................................38

4.4    Organizational structures model............................................... 40

4.5    Skills and competencies model..................................................43

4.6    Principles and policies model ................................................... 44

4.7    Culture, ethics, and behavior model ..........................................45

4.8    Service capabilities model ........................................................ 46


**5      The process model** ..................................................................... **49**

5.1    The process model .....................................................................49

5.2    Governance and management processes ....................................53

5.3    Process reference model ............................................................53

5.4    Process reference guide .............................................................55

5.5    Governance Domain: Evaluate, Direct, & Monitor....................57

        EDM01: Ensure governance framework setting and maintenance......58

        EDM02: Ensure benefits delivery..............................................58

        EDM03: Ensure Risk Optimization ...........................................59

        EDM04: Ensure Resource Optimization ....................................59

        EDM05: Ensure Stakeholder Transparency............................. 60

5.6    Management Domain: Align, Plan, & Organize ....................... 60

        APO01: Manage the IT management framework .......................61

        APO02: Manage strategy.............................................................61

        APO03: Manage Enterprise Architecture ..................................62

        APO04: Manage Innovation........................................................62

APO05: Manage Portfolio ...................................................63
APO06: Manage Budget, and Costs .....................................63
APO07: Manage Human Resources ......................................64
APO08: Manage Relationships .............................................64
APO09: Manage Service Agreements ...................................65
APO10: Manage Suppliers ....................................................65
APO11: Manage Quality .......................................................66
APO12: Manage Risk ............................................................66
APO13: Manage Security.......................................................67
5.7  Management Domain: Build, Acquire & Implement..............67
BAI01: Manage Programs and Projects.................................68
BAI02: Manage requirements definition ...............................68
BAI03: Manage solutions identification and build................69
BAI04: Manage Availability & Capacity...............................69
BAI05: Manage organizational change enablement................70
BAI06: Manage Changes .......................................................70
BAI07: Manage change acceptance and transitioning...........71
BAI08: Manage Knowledge...................................................71
BAI09: Manage Assets...........................................................72
BAI10: Manage Configuration..............................................72
5.8  Management Domain: Deliver, Service & Support...............73
DSS01: Manage Operations...................................................73
DSS02: Manage Service Requests and Incidents..................73
DSS03: Manage Problems......................................................74
DSS04: Manage Continuity ..................................................74
DSS05: Manage Security Services ........................................75
DSS06: Manage Business Process Controls ..........................75
5.9  Management Domain: Monitor, Evaluate & Assure..............76
MEA01: Monitor, evaluate and assess performance and
conformance..........................................................................76
MEA02: Monitor, evaluate and assess the system of internal control.76
MEA03: Monitor, evaluate and assess compliance with external
requirements .........................................................................77

6      Implementation guidance.................................................... 79
6.1    Introduction...................................................................79
6.2    Considering the IT organization context .......................... 80
6.3    Creating the right environment .......................................81

6.4    Recognizing pain-points and event triggers ................................. 82
6.5    Enabling change .............................................................................. 83
6.6    A lifecycle approach........................................................................ 83
6.7    Getting started: making the business case...................................... 85

**7      The process capability model............................................................ 87**
7.1    Introduction...................................................................................... 87
7.2    Benefits of the changes ................................................................... 90
7.3    Performing process capability assessments .................................... 90

**Appendices**
A      Detailed mappings ........................................................................... 93
B      Stakeholder needs and enterprise goals ........................................... 99
C      COBIT 5 vs. COBIT 4.1 ................................................................105
D      COBIT 5 and ITGI's five governance focus areas....................... 107
E      Mapping between COBIT 5 and legacy ISACA frameworks .........109
F      About ISACA® ..............................................................................119

# List of figures

Figure 2.1 – COBIT 5 principles ...............................................................9
Figure 2.2 – Architecture ........................................................................11
Figure 2.3 – The governance objective: value creation ...........................12
Figure 2.4 – Governance roles, activities, and relationships ...................13
Figure 2.5 – Governance in COBIT 5 ......................................................13
Figure 2.6 – Enablers: systemic model with interacting enablers ...........17
Figure 2.7 – Generic enabler model .........................................................17
Figure 2.8 – Generic enabler capability model.........................................18

Figure 3.1 – Goals cascade overview ...................................................... 22

Figure 4.1 – Generic enabler model..........................................................35
Figure 4.2 – Process model.......................................................................36
Figure 4.3 – Metadata: information cycle .................................................37
Figure 4.4 – Information model.................................................................38
Figure 4.5 – Organizational structures model.......................................... 40
Figure 4.6 – Skills and competencies model ............................................43
Figure 4.7 – Principles and policies model............................................... 44
Figure 4.8 – Culture, ethics, and behavior model ....................................45
Figure 4.9 – Service capabilities model ................................................... 46

Figure 5.1 – The process model revisited .................................................50
Figure 5.2 – Governance and management processes................................53
Figure 5.3 – Illustrative governance and management processes..............55

Figure 6.1 – The seven phases of the implementation lifecycle .............. 85

Figure 7.1 – Summary of the COBIT 4.1 process maturity model ........... 88
Figure 7.2 – Summary of the COBIT 5 process capability model............89

Figure E1 – Legacy governance of enterprise IT focus areas ................107

# List of tables

Table 1.1 – Various frameworks .............................................................................7

Table 2.1 – Stakeholder needs.............................................................................15
Table 2.2 – Governance and management interactions ....................................... 20

Table 3.1 – Enterprise goals mapped to governance objectives........................... 23
Table 3.2 – IT-related goals................................................................................. 24
Table 3.3 – Enterprise goal sample metrics ......................................................... 26
Table 3.4 – IT-related goal sample metrics.......................................................... 28
Table 3.5 – Benefits.............................................................................................32

Table 4.1 – Roles and organizational structures ..................................................41
Table 4.2 – Skills categories ............................................................................... 44

Table B1 – Mapping COBIT 5 enterprise goals to IT-related goals......................95
Table B2 – Mapping COBIT 5 IT-related goals to COBIT 5 processes .............. 97

Table C1 – Mapping COBIT 5 enterprise goals to typical stakeholder needs... 100
Table C2 – Mapping COBIT 5 IT-related goals to typical stakeholder needs....102

Table E1 – Coverage of governance focus areas ................................................108

Table F1 – COBIT 4.1 control objectives mapped to COBIT 5...........................109
Table F2 – Val IT 2.0 key management practices covered by COBIT 5 .............115
Table F3 – Risk IT key management practices covered by COBIT 5 .................117

# CHAPTER 1

# Introduction and executive summary

## 1.1 Introduction

Information is a key resource for all enterprises, and throughout the whole lifecycle of information there is a huge dependency on technology. Information and related information technologies are pervasive in enterprises and they need to be governed and managed in a holistic manner, taking in the full end-to-end business and IT functional areas of responsibility.

Today, more than ever, enterprises need to achieve increased:
- Value creation throughout the enterprise's IT
- Business user satisfaction with IT engagement and services
- Compliance with relevant laws, regulations and policies

COBIT 5 is a governance and management framework for information and related technology that starts from stakeholder needs with regard to information and technology. The framework is intended for all enterprises, including non-profit and public sector.

Several global business catastrophes over the last few decades such as the Asian financial crisis of 1997[1], the early 2000s recession (2001 to 2003 – the collapse

---

[1] www.stocktradingtogo.com/2008/07/18/timeline-of-all-recessions-and-world-crises-since-great-depression/

of the Dot Com Bubble, September 11th attacks and accounting scandals)[2], the
ENRON scandal[3], and the banking collapses of 2008 to 2012[4], have brought the
term "governance" to the forefront of business thinking. On the positive side, some
success stories have also demonstrated the importance of good governance. Both
have established a clear and widely accepted need for more rigorous governance.
Increasingly, legislation is being passed and regulations implemented to address
this need, which has moved governance to the top of agendas at all levels of the
enterprise.

The COBIT framework allows enterprises to achieve their governance and
management objectives, i.e., to create optimal value from information and
technology by maintaining a balance amongst realizing benefits, managing risk
and balancing resources. Further benefits include but are not limited to:
- Maintain high-quality information to support business decisions
- Achieve strategic goals and realize business benefits through the effective and
  innovative use of IT
- Achieve operational excellence through reliable, efficient application of
  technology
- Maintain IT-related risk at an acceptable level
- Optimize the cost of IT services and technology
- Support compliance with relevant laws, regulations, contractual agreements
  and policies

## 1.2   What is governance of enterprise IT?

There are many sources competing to be the definitive authority on this topic. Here
are a few examples. For the purpose of this publication 'governance of enterprise
IT' is used as a short form for "*the governance of enterprise IT*".

### CIO Magazine[5]
*Governance of enterprise IT is putting in place a structure aligning the IT strategy
with the business strategy. This enables enterprises in staying the course in achieving
their strategies and goals, as well as implementing proper means of measuring*

---

2   www.stocktradingtogo.com/2008/07/18/timeline-of-all-recessions-and-world-crises-since-
    great-depression/
3   http://www.oecd.org/daf/corporateaffairs/corporategovernanceprinciples/35639607.pdf
4   news.bbc.co.uk
5   Based on the definition found at www.cio.com

*the performance of the IT enterprise. Governance of enterprise IT takes into consideration the interests of all stakeholders and ensures that processes provide measurable results. A governance of enterprise IT framework should answer some key questions, such as:*

- *What are the key metrics needed by the management team?*
- *How well is the IT enterprise functioning?*
- *What is the return on investment to the business of investing in IT?*

## Enterprise for Economic Co-operation and Development (OECD)[6]

*Governance of enterprise IT is the set of processes and procedures to direct and control an enterprise. The corporate governance structure specifies the distribution of rights and responsibilities among the different participants in the enterprise – such as the board, managers, shareholders and other stakeholders – and lays down the rules and procedures for decision-making.*

## BWISE[7]

*Governance of enterprise IT is a subset of an enterprise's corporate governance strategy. Governance of enterprise IT focuses specifically on information technology systems, their performance, and risk management. The primary goals of governance of enterprise IT are to assure that the investments in IT generate business value, and to mitigate the risks that are associated with IT.*

## ISACA[8]

*Governance ensures that stakeholder needs, conditions, and options are evaluated to determine balanced, agreed-on enterprise objectives to be achieved; setting direction through prioritization and decision making; and monitoring performance and compliance against agreed-on direction and objectives.*

*COBIT 5 provides an end-to-end business view of the governance of enterprise IT that reflects the central role of information and technology in creating value for enterprises. The principles, practices, analytical tools and models found in COBIT 5 embody thought leadership and guidance from business, IT and governance experts around the world.*

---

6   Based on the definition found at www.oecd.org
7   Based on the definition found at www.bwise.com
8   Based on the definition found in the glossary at www.isaca.org

## Compliance

Governance and compliance are not synonymous. Basically compliance can be summarized as *the state or fact of according with or meeting rules or standards.* Synonyms include: agreement, consent, accord, accordance, and conformity.

**What are the major focus areas that make up governance of enterprise IT?**

According to the IT Governance Institute[9], there are five areas of focus:

1. **Strategic alignment**

    This covers the alignment of the enterprise's and IT's perspective, position, plans, and patterns.

2. **Value delivery**

    From a customer perspective, value is expressed in terms of the desired business outcomes, their preferences, and their perceptions in regards to the product or service.

3. **Resource management**

    It is important to include the following elements as resources: funding, applications/software, infrastructure/hardware, information/data, and of course people. In order to properly manage their resources, enterprises must develop and maintain the following capabilities: management, enterprise, processes, knowledge, and people.

4. **Risk management**

    A risk may be defined as the uncertainty of an outcome whether positive or negative. The management of the risk includes the identification of the tangible and intangible items to be protected, the various (real or potential) threats facing those items and the level of vulnerability of the items in regards to a specific threat. The enterprise must then decide an appropriate means of mitigating the risk; this may range from doing nothing to attempting to fully protect the item from the threat.

5. **Performance measures**

    Before establishing any measure an enterprise needs to identify the reason for the measure. There are four basic reasons for measuring: they are to direct, to validate, to justify, and to intervene. The enterprise needs to identify many

---

9   Based on the definition found at http://www.isaca.org/Pages/Glossary.aspx?tid=422&char=G

other criteria for the measures. These criteria include, but are not limited to, compliance, performance, quality, and value. Furthermore, the measures can be quantitative (objective) or qualitative (subjective). All the measures must also adhere to the SMART principle where

**S** = Specific
**M** = Measurable
**A** = Achievable
**R** = Realistic
**T** = Timely or time bounded

Evidently, there is much more regarding the above. However, as this publication is only a management guide about governance of enterprise IT, the reader is invited to consult Appendix A for a list of websites and books for further details and explanations.

The topics of governance and compliance (sometimes known as *"transparency"*) are now common in various books, whitepapers, articles, conference presentations, and blogs. To make good governance happen and deliver the expected results, enterprises must address the challenge of participation. It's all about the attitude, the behavior, and the culture of the enterprise[10].

One of the primary behaviors that the management team of the IT enterprise needs to encourage is the broad on-going participation of all IT stakeholders to ensure that governance of enterprise IT makes a significant and visible contribution.

Corporate governance is critical for ensuring that key decisions are consistent with corporate vision, values, and strategy. The same can be said about governance of enterprise IT. However, this can only be accomplished if the IT enterprise derives its vision, values, and strategy from the corporate ones.

According to the CIO Magazine[11], the IT enterprise makes five types of business-related decisions
1. IT principles and policies to drive the role of IT in the enterprise
2. IT architecture based on existing and future technical choices and directions
3. IT infrastructure for the delivery of shared IT services

---

10 ABC of ICT
11 www.cio.com

4. Business application requirements for each project
5. Prioritization of IT investments based on business priorities

Enterprises need to design, transition, and operate governance mechanisms to make and then implement each of the above types of decisions. There are many types of governance mechanisms and techniques:
• Mechanisms that facilitate decision making
• Processes that ensure alignment between technology and business goals
• Methods for communicating governance principles and decisions

In order to accomplish the above, the executive team (corporate and IT) should:
• Set the IT priorities
• Communicate priorities and progress clearly and regularly
• Monitor projects regularly

## 1.3   Overview of this publication

This publication provides an explanation of the objectives, scope and format of COBIT 5, and introduces the COBIT 5 architecture. It allows various stakeholders to understand how COBIT 5 meets the stakeholder needs for governance and management of enterprise IT and how it can be used, and it provides implementation guidance. Further sections of the document are:

1. Introduction and executive summary
2. The COBIT 5 principles
3. The goals cascade
4. Detailed description of the enabler models
5. The process model
6. Implementation guidance
7. The process capability model

## 1.4   What to use? Where to start?

There is an old adage that says that "*it doesn't make sense to reinvent the wheel*". There are many existing and well documented complementary frameworks and methodologies which can be used. All have been designed, implemented, and used by a worldwide community of enterprises and industry experts.

Table 1.1 Various frameworks

| | |
|---|---|
| **COBIT** | The framework, from the Information Systems Audit and Control Association (ISACA), is probably the most popular. It is a set of guidelines and supporting toolset for governance of enterprise IT that is accepted worldwide. Auditors and enterprises use it as a mechanism to integrate technology in implementing controls and meet specific business objectives. COBIT is well suited to enterprises focused on risk management and mitigation. |
| **ITIL** | ITIL advocates that IT services must be aligned to the needs of the business and underpin the core business processes. It provides guidance to enterprises on how to use IT effectively and efficiently as a tool to facilitate business change, transformation, and growth. There are five core publications which provide a systematic and professional approach to the management of IT services, enabling enterprises to deliver appropriate services and continually ensure they are meeting business goals and delivering benefits. |
| **COSO** | This model for evaluating internal controls is from the Committee of Sponsoring Enterprises of the Treadway Commission. It includes guidelines on many functions, including human resource management, inbound and outbound logistics, external resources, information technology, risk, legal affairs, the enterprise, marketing and sales, operations, all financial functions, procurement and reporting. This is a more business-general framework that is less IT-specific than COBIT or ITIL. |
| **CMMI** | The Capability Maturity Model Integration method, created by a group from government, industry and Carnegie-Mellon's Software Engineering Institute, is a process improvement approach that contains 22 process areas. It is divided into appraisal, evaluation, and structure. CMMI is particularly well suited to enterprises that need help with application development, lifecycle issues, and improving the delivery of products throughout the lifecycle. |

## What can go wrong if it's not implemented effectively?

If the governance of enterprise IT framework isn't implemented properly, it can directly affect how IT is perceived by the business and other high-level stakeholders. Ineffective implementation of the governance of enterprise IT can exacerbate already on-going issues such as project overruns and poor value to cost measurements, not to mention stakeholder dissatisfaction.

Complying with governance of enterprise IT represents a myriad of challenges. Some of these challenges include, but are not limited to

- IT personnel not informed of the requirements of compliance
- Not having IT controls in place
- Missing a deadline or reporting a "material weakness" in your IT controls

## 1.5  Implementation tips

The following list represent "must-have" to ensure a (relatively) smooth implementation as well as the positive delivery of expected results. The following approach, often referred to as *Kotter's[12] Eight-Steps to transformation* is widely known and well documented.

1.  Create a sense of urgency
2.  Form a guiding coalition
3.  Create a vision
4.  Communicate the vision
5.  Empower others to act on the vision
6.  Plan for and create quick wins
7.  Consolidate improvements and produce more change
8.  Institutionalize the change

## 1.6  Appendices

Appendices contain reference information, mappings and more detailed information on specific subjects:

Appendix A – References
Appendix B – Detailed mappings
Appendix C – Stakeholder needs and enterprise goals
Appendix D – COBIT 5 vs. COBIT 4.1
Appendix E – COBIT 5 and the IT Governance Institute's (ITGI) five governance focus areas
Appendix F – Mapping between COBIT 5 and legacy ISACA frameworks
Appendix G – About ISACA

---

12 Leading Change: Why Transformation Efforts Fail, Kotter John P, Harvard Business Review March-April 1995

# CHAPTER 2

# The COBIT 5 principles

The framework covers the whole enterprise providing a basis to integrate effectively other frameworks, standards, and practices used. The framework is made up of a single overarching one, allowing for a consistent and integrated source of guidance in a non-technical, technology-independent common language.

The framework is based on the following principles, see figure 2.1.

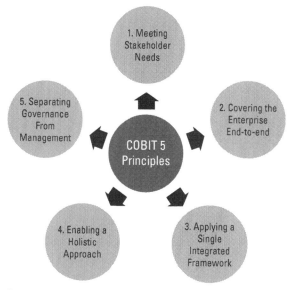

Figure 2.1  COBIT 5 principles

The framework integrates all knowledge previously dispersed over different ISACA frameworks[13] such as COBIT, Val IT, Risk IT, and the Business Model for Information Security (BMIS) and the IT Assurance Framework (ITAF).

The benefit of the architecture within the framework is to support the goals, i.e., providing to all stakeholders the most complete and up-to-date guidance on governance and management of the enterprise's IT.

Figure 2.2 provides a graphical description of the COBIT 5 architecture that result from this principle.

## 2.1   Principle 1: Meeting Stakeholder Needs

COBIT 5 is an integrator framework because it:
- Brings together existing ISACA[14] guidance on governance and management of the enterprise's IT
- Aligns with the latest versions of relevant standards and frameworks[15]
- Provides a simple architecture for structuring guidance materials and producing a consistent product set

## 2.2   Principle 2: Covering the enterprise end-to-end

Enterprises exist to create value for their stakeholders, so the governance objective for any enterprise – commercial or not – is value creation. Value creation is based on the customer's perceptions, preferences, and desired business outcomes. It means realizing benefits at an optimal resource cost while optimizing risk (see Figure 2.3). Enterprises have many stakeholders, and "creating value" means different things to each of them – sometimes conflicting. Governance is about negotiating and deciding the value interests amongst different stakeholders. By consequence, the governance system must consider all stakeholders when making assessments and decisions about benefit, resource, and risk. For each of these value creation components, the question can and should be asked: for who are the benefits, and risk, and which resources are required?

---

13  See www.isaca.org for more details on each of these frameworks
14  See Appendix G – About ISACA
15  Such as ITIL®, ISO/IEC 20000®, ISO/IEC 27000®, ISO/IEC 31000®, PMI's PMBOK® for example

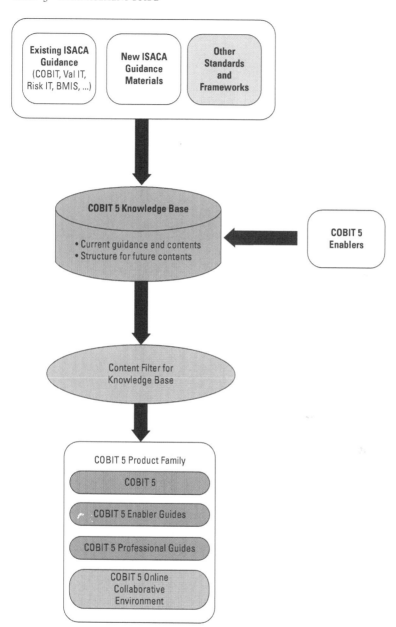

Figure 2.2 Architecture

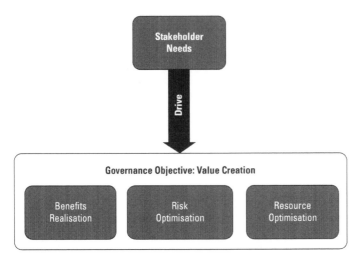

Figure 2.3 The governance objective: value creation
Source: Figure 3: The Governance Objective: Value Creation, COBIT 5: A Business Framework for the Governance and Management of Enterprise IT, 2012 © ISACA.

In addition to the governance objective, the other three main elements of the governance approach include the following.

## Governance enablers
These are the organizational resources for governance, such as frameworks, principles, structure, processes, and practices, toward which (or through which) action is directed and objectives can be attained. Enablers also include the enterprise's resources (people, funding, applications, infrastructures, and information) and service capabilities (management, enterprise, process, knowledge, and people).

## Governance scope
Governance can be applied to the whole enterprise, an entity, a tangible or intangible asset, anything that requires governance. It is possible to define different views of the enterprise to which governance is applied, and it is essential to define this scope of the governance system well.

## Roles, activities and relationships
Lastly, we have the governance roles, activities, and relationships. It defines who is involved in governance, how they are involved, what they do, and how they interact, within the scope of any governance system. In the governance and management domains, there is a clear differentiation between governance and management

activities, interfaces and roles. Figure 2.4[16] builds on the previous figure (see Figure 2.3), by including the interactions between the different roles.

Figure 2.4 Governance roles, activities, and relationships
Source: Figure 9: Key Roles, Activities and Relationships, COBIT 5: A Business Framework for the Governance and Management of Enterprise IT, 2012 © ISACA.

Figure 2.5 (Governance in COBIT 5) represents the key components of a governance system.[17]

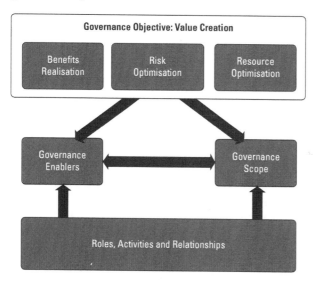

Figure 2.5 Governance in COBIT 5
Source: Figure 8: Governance and Management in COBIT 5: A Business Framework for the Governance and Management of Enterprise IT, 2012 © ISACA

---

16 COBIT 5: The Framework Exposure Draft (June 2011)
17 This governance system is an illustration of ISACA's Taking Governance Forward (TGF) initiative; more information on TGF can be found on page www.takinggovernanceforward. org/Pages/default.aspx

## 2.3   Principle 3: Applying a Single, Integrated Framework

COBIT 5 addresses the governance and management of information and related technology from an enterprise-wide, end-to-end perspective, including the activities and responsibilities of both the IT function and non-IT business functions. The end-to-end aspect is further supported by the framework's coverage of all critical business elements, i.e. processes, organizational structures, principles and policies, culture, skills, and service capabilities. In addition, an information model provides a simple link between business information and the IT function, which further supports the business focus.

Every enterprise operates in a different context; this context is determined by external factors (market, industry, geopolitical, etc.) and internal factors (culture, enterprise, risk appetite, etc.), and requires that every enterprise builds their own, customized governance and management system. The structure of COBIT 5, the governance and management model, and the enabler models apply to all contexts and facilitate this customization. For example:
- The goals cascade is the mechanism to translate context specific business drivers and stakeholder needs into specific, actionable and customized IT related and enabler goals
- Quality goals associated with each enabler are to a large extent contextual

The framework achieves a business focus by identifying all stakeholders and their needs and determining how they link to governance and management decisions and activities. In this section, the typical internal and external stakeholders for information and related technology in the enterprise are described first, along with some of their typical issues and concerns.

### Stakeholders and stakeholder needs
The needs of stakeholders are influenced by many drivers such as changes in strategy, changes in business and regulatory environment, and making use of new technologies. The needs of stakeholder materialize in a series of potential expectations, concerns, or requirements. These relate to one or more of the three generic governance objectives within the framework: benefits realization, risk balancing and cost optimization.

Stakeholders for information and related technology can be external and internal, and they can have many different and sometimes conflicting needs – as shown in Table 2.1.

Table 2.1  Stakeholder needs

| Internal stakeholders | Internal stakeholder needs |
|---|---|
| Board, CEO, chief financial officer (CFO), chief information officer (CIO), business executives, business process owners, business managers, risk managers, security managers, service managers, HR managers, internal audit, privacy officers, IT users, IT managers, etc. | • How do I get value from IT?<br>• How do I manage performance of IT?<br>• How can I best exploit new technology for new strategic opportunities?<br>• How do I know whether I'm compliant with all applicable regulations?<br>• How do I best build and structure my IT department?<br>• What are (control) requirements for Information?<br>• Did I address all IT-related risks?<br>• Am I running an efficient and resilient IT operation?<br>• How do I control cost of IT? How do I use IT resources in the most effective and efficient manner? What are the most effective and efficient sourcing options?<br>• Do I have enough people for IT? How do I develop and maintain their skills, and how do I manage their performance?<br>• How do I get assurance over IT?<br>• Is the information I am processing well secured?<br>• How do I improve business agility through a more flexible IT environment?<br>• Is it clear what IT is doing?<br>• How often do IT projects fail to deliver what they promised?<br>• How critical is IT to sustaining the enterprise? |
| External stakeholders | External stakeholder needs |
| Business partners, suppliers, shareholders, regulators/government, external users, customers, standardization enterprises, external auditors, consultants, etc. | • How do I know my business partner's operations are secure and reliable?<br>• How do I know the enterprise is compliant with applicable rules and regulations?<br>• How do I know the enterprise is maintaining an effective system of internal control? |

# 2.4  Principle 4: Enabling a Holistic Approach

The purpose of an enabler is to implement an effective governance and management system for the enterprise's IT. An enabler is broadly defined as anything that can assist in achieving the governance objectives of the enterprise. This includes resources, such as funding, applications, infrastructure, information, and people. Enablers interact in a systemic way, meaning that a governance and management system cannot succeed unless all enablers are dealt with and the major interactions are understood. The framework lists seven categories of enablers:

- Principles, policies, and frameworks
- Processes
- Organizational structures
- Culture, ethics, and behavior
- Information
- Services, infrastructure and applications
- People, skills, and competencies

### Enablers

These are the tangible and intangible elements that make something work – in this case, governance, and management of the enterprise over IT. Enablers are driven by the goals cascade described later in this book: the higher-level IT-related goals define what the different enablers should achieve.

### Systemic governance

When dealing with governance of enterprise IT, good decisions, and enterprise should take into account the systemic nature of governance arrangements. All interrelated enablers are analyzed and addressed to meet the needs of the various stakeholders.

Figure 2.6 shows the seven categories of enablers and the fact that they are all interconnected. This interconnection represents the mind-set an enterprise should adopt for enterprise governance, which includes governance of enterprise IT. In order to achieve its main objective an enterprise must always consider an interconnected set of enablers. An enabler:

- Needs the input of other enablers to be fully effective (e.g., processes need information, organizational structures need people, people need skills and behavior, and *vice versa*)
- Delivers output to the benefit of other enablers, e.g., processes deliver information, skills, and behavior make processes efficient

### The generic enabler model

All enablers have certain common elements. Because a governance system is a complex interaction amongst all enablers, having a simple, structured, and uniform enabler model can facilitate both adoption and successful execution. This model is a key component of the framework as it represents the basic structure for all seven categories of enablers. The generic enabler model identifies a number of common components:

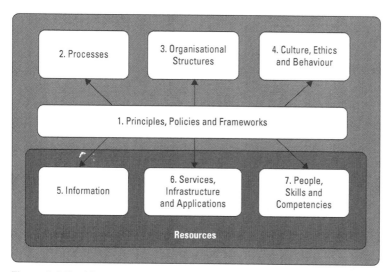

Figure 2.6  Enablers: systemic model with interacting enablers
Source: Figure 12: COBIT 5 Enterprise Enablers in COBIT 5: A Business Framework for the Governance and
Management of Enterprise IT, 2012 © ISACA.

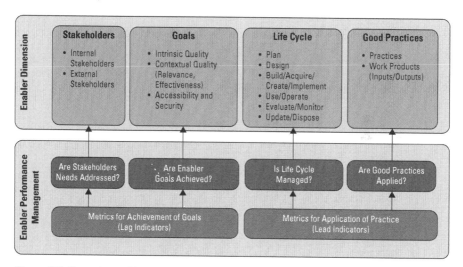

Figure 2.7  Generic enabler model
Source: Figure 13: COBIT 5 Enablers: Generic, COBIT 5: A Business Framework for the Governance and
Management of Enterprise IT, 2012 © ISACA.

- Stakeholders
- Goals and metrics
- Life cycle
- Good practice
- Attributes

Figure 2.7 shows the overall generic structure of the COBIT 5 enablers.

### The capability attribute for enablers

The model makes a distinction between:

- The basic capability level (Level 1-Performed), which indicates that an enabler is generally achieving its stated goals, and that enabler good practices are to a large extent applied. These two criteria – achieving goals and applying good practice – are the attribute of the performed level
- More advanced capability levels, indicating increasing levels of sophistication in the enabler, providing greater efficiency, formalization, control, optimization etc. These advanced capability levels are expressed using a scale from 2 to 5[18], and for each of these levels a number of attributes will need to be achieved. These attributes are different between enablers and need to be defined per enabler.

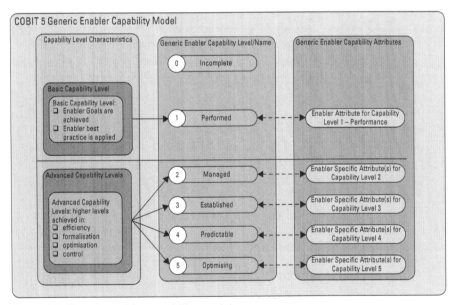

Figure 2.8  Generic enabler capability model

---

18 This scale, with the names of the different levels, is taken from ISO/IEC 15504

The generic capability attribute model is based on the principles of ISO/IEC 15504, which is a process capability assessment model, see figure 2.8.

## 2.5 Principle 5: Separating Governance from Management

Governance and management are very different types of activities that require different organizational structures, and serve different purposes. In every enterprise, multiple stakeholders have different and sometimes conflicting perceptions of benefits, risk, and resources. This creates a need for clarity on what should be done and how it should be done to meet the stakeholder objectives.

In summary, the disciplines of governance and management include different types of activities, require different organizational structures, and serve different purposes.

The framework makes a clear distinction between governance and management. As this distinction is fundamental to the framework, the following sections explain the framework's view of governance and management.

### Governance system

A governance system refers to all the methods and techniques that enable multiple stakeholders in an enterprise to have an organized say in evaluating conditions and options; setting direction; and monitoring compliance, performance, and progress against plans, to satisfy specific enterprise objectives. Methods and techniques include frameworks, principles, policies, sponsorship, structures and decision tools, roles and responsibilities, processes and practices, to set direction and monitor compliance and performance aligned with the overall objectives. In most enterprises, this is the responsibility of the board of directors under the leadership of the chief executive officer (CEO) and chairperson.

### Management

Management entails the considered use of means (resources, people, processes, practices, etc.) to achieve an identified end. It is through management that the governance body achieves a result or objective. Management is responsible for the execution of the direction set by the guiding body or unit. Management is about planning, building, organizing and controlling operational activities to align with the direction set by the governance body.

**Interactions between governance and management**

The above definitions of governance and management make it clear they are different types of activities, with different responsibilities. Given the role of governance which is to evaluate, direct, and monitor, a set of interactions is required between governance and management to result in an efficient and effective governance system. These interactions, using the enabler structure, include those shown in Table 2.2.

Table 2.2 Governance and management interactions

| Enabler | Governance-Management Interaction |
|---------|-----------------------------------|
| Process | In the illustrative COBIT 5 process model (COBIT 5: Enabling Processes), a distinction is made between governance and management processes, including specific sets of practices and activities for each. The process model also includes RACI charts, describing the responsibilities of different organisational structures and roles within the enterprise. |
| Information | The process model describes inputs to and outputs from the different process practices to other processes, including information exchanged between governance and management processes. Information used for evaluating, directing, and monitoring enterprise IT is exchanged between governance and management as described in the process model inputs and outputs. |
| Organizational structures | A number of organisational structures are defined in each enterprise; structures can sit in the governance space or the management space, depending on their composition and scope of decisions. Because governance is about setting the direction, interaction takes place between the decisions taken by the governance structures, e.g.: deciding about the investment portfolio and setting risk appetite and the decisions and operations implementing the former. |
| Principles, policies and framework | Principles, policies and frameworks are the vehicle by which governance decisions are institutionalised within the enterprise, and for that reason are an interaction between governance decisions (direction setting) and management (execution of decisions). |
| Culture, ethics & behavior | Behavior is also a key enabler of good governance and management of the enterprise. It is set at the top – leading by example – and is therefore an important interaction between governance and management. |
| People, skills, & competencies | Governance and management activities require different skill sets, but an essential skill for both governance body members and management is to understand both tasks and how they are different. |
| Services, infrastructure and applications | Services are required, supported by applications and infrastructure to provide the governance body with adequate information and to support the governance activities of evaluating, setting direction, and monitoring. |

# CHAPTER 3

# The goals cascade

## Introduction

The *goals cascade* translates stakeholder needs into governance objective and enterprise goals, and then further down to IT-related goals, processes, and process goals. This cascade is shown in Figure 3.1.

The cascade applies to every enterprise – for-profit, non-profit, government departments and agencies, etc. The goals cascade is the mechanism that translates stakeholder concerns into tangible goals that can be managed in a more consistent manner. This cascade can be described systematically as follows.

**Step #1 Stakeholder needs to governance objectives**

Stakeholder needs, which are influenced by a number of drivers, can be related to one or more of the governance objectives of benefits delivery, risk balancing, and cost optimization.

**Step #2 Governance objectives to enterprise goals**

Overall governance objectives for the enterprise translate into, and map onto a set of generic enterprise goals; these enterprise goals have been developed using the Balanced Scorecard (BSC)[19] dimensions and they represent a list of commonly used goals an enterprise has defined for

---

19 Kaplan, Robert S.; David P. Norton; The Balanced Scorecard: Translating Strategy into Action; Harvard University Press, USA, 1996

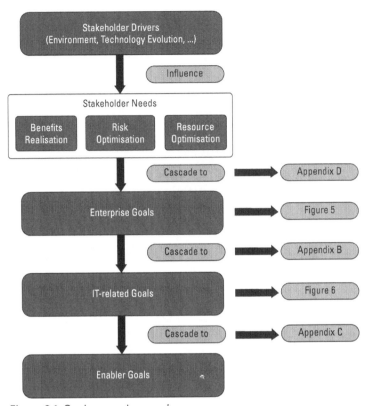

**Figure 3.1 Goals cascade overview**
Source: Figure 4: COBIT 5 Goals Cascade Overview, COBIT 5: A Business Framework for the Governance and
Management of Enterprise IT, 2012 © ISACA.

itself. Although this list is not exhaustive, most enterprise-specific goals can be easily mapped onto one or more of the generic enterprise goals. The framework defines 17 generic goals (as shown in Table 3.1), which list the enterprise goals, and how they relate to the governance objectives.

The framework uses two types of relationships: primary and secondary. A relationship deemed primary is a strong and direct one. A relationship deemed secondary is not as strong and may be indirect. In the mapping table below, a "**P**" stands for primary relationship, and an "**S**" for secondary relationship.

## Table 3.1 Enterprise goals mapped to governance objectives

Source Figure 22: COBIT 5, A Business Framework for the Governance and Management of Enterprise IT, 2012 © ISACA.

| BSC Dimension | Enterprise goals | Governance objectives | | |
| --- | --- | --- | --- | --- |
| | | Benefits realization | Risk management | Resource optimization |
| Financial | 1. Stakeholder value of business investments | P | | |
| | 2. Portfolio of competitive products, and services | P | P | S |
| | 3. Managed business risks (safeguarding of assets) | | P | S |
| | 4. Compliance with external laws, and regulations | | P | |
| | 5. Financial transparency | P | S | S |
| Customer | 6. Customer-oriented service culture | P | | S |
| | 7. Business service continuity and availability | | P | |
| | 8. Agile responses to a changing business environment | P | | S |
| | 9. Information-based strategic decision making | P | P | P |
| | 10. Optimization of service delivery costs | P | | P |
| Internal | 11. Optimization of business process functionality | P | | P |
| | 12. Optimization of business process costs | P | | P |
| | 13. Managed business change programs | P | P | S |
| | 14. Operational, and staff productivity | P | | P |
| | 15. Compliance with internal policies | | P | |
| Learning and growth | 16. Skilled, and motivated people | S | P | P |
| | 17. Product and business innovation culture | P | | |

## Step #3  Enterprise goals to IT-related goals

Realizing enterprise goals requires a number of IT-related outcomes;[2] these IT-related outcomes are represented by the IT-related goals, which are also a set of generic goals (related to IT) for business departments, and for IT. The framework defines 17 IT-related goals as listed in Table 3.2.

Table 3.2 IT-related goals

Source Figure 22: COBIT 5, A Business Framework for the Governance and Management of Enterprise IT, 2012
© ISACA.

| IT-related goals | | |
|---|---|---|
| Financial | 1. | Alignment of it, and business strategy |
| | 2. | IT compliance, and support for business compliance with external laws, and regulations |
| | 3. | Commitment of executive management for making it-related decisions |
| | 4. | Managed it-related business risks |
| | 5. | Realized benefits from it-enabled investments, and services portfolio |
| | 6. | Transparency of IT costs, benefits, and risks |
| Customer | 7. | Delivery of IT services in line with business requirements |
| | 8. | Adequate usage of applications, information, and technology solutions |
| Internal | 9. | IT agility |
| | 10. | Security of information, and processing infrastructure, and applications |
| | 11. | Optimization of IT assets, resources, and capabilities |
| | 12. | Enablement and support of business processes by integrating applications, and technology into business processes |
| | 13. | Delivery of programs on time, on budget, and meeting requirements, and quality standards |
| | 14. | Availability of reliable and useful information |
| | 15. | IT compliance with internal policies |
| Learning and growth | 16. | Competent and motivated IT personnel |
| | 17. | Knowledge, expertise, and initiatives for business innovation |

## Step #4  IT-related goals to enabler goals

IT-related goals require the successful application and use of a number of enablers to be achieved. Enablers include processes, organizational structures, and information. For each enabler there is a set of goals defined in support of the IT-related goals.

## 3.1   Using the goals cascade

### Benefits of the goals cascade

The goals cascade is important because it allows the definition of priorities for implementation, improvement, and assurance of the enterprise's governance of IT, based on (strategic) objectives of the enterprise[20]. In practice, the goals cascade:

---

20 Source: COBIT 5 Enabling Processes, page 15

- Defines relevant, and tangible goals, and objectives at various levels of responsibility
- Filters the knowledge base of the framework based on enterprise goals, to extract relevant guidance for inclusion in specific implementation, improvement, or assurance projects
- Clearly identifies, and communicates how (sometimes very operational) enablers are important to achieve enterprise goals

> The goals cascade is based on research performed by the University of Antwerp Management School (UAMS) IT Alignment, and Governance Institute in Belgium.[20]

## Using the goals cascade carefully[21]

The goals cascade provides mapping tables between enterprise goals and IT-related goals and between IT-related goals and the framework processes; but it does not contain the ultimate and most complete answer. Users of the framework should not attempt to use it in a purely literal way, but rather as a guideline. There are various reasons for this, including:

- Enterprises have different priorities and goals that usually change over time
- No distinction is made allowing for the enterprise size and industry
- They represent a sort of common denominator of how, in general, the different levels of goals are inter-related
- Because they use two levels of importance or relevancy, the mapping indicators seem to suggest these are "discrete" levels. In reality, the mapping is closer to a continuum of various degrees of relevancy

When using the goals cascade an enterprise should first customize the mapping, taking into account its specific situation:

- Strategic priorities, translated into a specific "weight" or importance for each of the enterprise goals
- A validation of the mappings of the goals cascade, taking into account the specific environment, industry, etc.

---

21 Source: COBIT 5 Enabling Processes, page 15
22 IT-related outcomes are obviously not the only intermediate benefit required to achieve enterprise goals. All other functional areas in an enterprise, such as finance, and marketing, also contribute to the achievement of enterprise goals, but within the context of COBIT 5 only IT-related activities and goals are considered.

## Table 3.3 Enterprise goal sample metrics

Source Figure 22: COBIT 5, A Business Framework for the Governance and Management of Enterprise IT, 2012
© ISACA.

| Bsc Dimensions | Enterprise goals | Metrics |
|---|---|---|
| Financial | 1. Compliance with external laws, and regulations | - Cost of regulatory non-compliance, including settlements, and fines<br>- Number of regulatory non-compliance issues causing public comment or negative publicity<br>- Number of regulatory non-compliance issues relating to contractual agreements with business partners |
| | 2. Managed business risks (safeguarding of assets) | - Percent of critical business objectives, and services covered by risk assessment<br>- Ratio of significant incidents that were not identified in risk assessments vs. total incidents<br>- Update frequency of risk profile |
| | 3. Portfolio of competitive products, and services | - Percent of products, and services that meet or exceed targets in revenues, and/or market share<br>- Ratio of products, and services per lifecycle phase<br>- Percent of products, and services that meet or exceed customer satisfaction targets<br>- Percent of products, and services that provide competitive advantage |
| | 4. Stakeholder value of business investments | - Percent of investments where value delivered meets stakeholder expectations<br>- Percent of products, and services where expected benefits realized<br>- Percent of investments where claimed benefits are met or exceeded |
| | 5. Financial transparency | - Percent of investment business cases with clearly defined, and approved expected costs, and benefits<br>- Percent of products, and services with defined, and approved operational costs, and expected benefits<br>- Satisfaction survey of key stakeholders regarding the transparency, understanding, and accuracy of enterprise financial information<br>- Percent of service cost that can be allocated to users |
| Customer | 6. Customer-oriented service culture | - Number of customer service disruptions due to it service-related incidents (reliability)<br>- Percent of business stakeholders satisfied that customer service delivery meets agreed-upon levels<br>- Number of customer complaints<br>- Trend of customer satisfaction survey results |
| | 7. Business service continuity and availability | - Number of customer service interruptions causing significant incidents<br>- Business cost of incidents<br>- Number of business processing hours lost due to unplanned service interruptions<br>- Percent of complaints as a function of committed service availability targets |

| Bsc Dimensions | Enterprise goals | Metrics |
|---|---|---|
| | 8. Agile responses to a changing business environment | - Level of board satisfaction with enterprise responsiveness to new requirements<br>- Number of critical products, and services supported by up-to-date business processes<br>- Average time to turn strategic enterprise objectives into an agreed and approved initiative |
| | 9. Information-based strategic decision making | - Degree of board, and executive management satisfaction with decision making<br>- Number of incidents caused by incorrect business decisions based on inaccurate information<br>- Time to provide supporting information to enable effective business decisions |
| | 10. Optimization of service delivery costs | - Frequency of service delivery cost optimization assessments<br>- Trend of cost assessment vs. service level results<br>- Satisfaction levels of board and executive management with service delivery costs internal |
| Internal | 11. Optimization of business process functionality | - Frequency of business process capability maturity assessments<br>- Trend of assessment results<br>- Satisfaction levels of board, and executives with business process capabilities |
| | 12. Optimization of business process costs | - Frequency of business process cost optimization assessments<br>- Trend of cost assessment vs. service level results<br>- Satisfaction levels of board and executive management with business processing costs |
| | 13. Managed business change programs | - Number of programs on time, and within budget<br>- Percent of stakeholders satisfied with program delivery<br>- Level of awareness of business change induced by it-enabled business initiatives |
| | 14. Operational and staff productivity | - Number of programs/projects on time, and within budget<br>- Cost and staffing levels compared to benchmarks |
| | 15. Compliance with internal policies | - Number of incidents related to non-compliance to policy<br>- Percent of stakeholders who understand policies<br>- Percent of policies supported by effective standards, and working practices<br>- Learning and growth |
| Learning and growth | 16. Skilled, and motivated people | - Level of stakeholder satisfaction with staff expertise, and skills<br>- Percent of staff whose skills are insufficient for the competency required for their role<br>- Percent of satisfied staff |
| | 17. Product and business innovation culture | - Level of awareness, and understanding of business innovation opportunities<br>- Stakeholder satisfaction with levels of product, and innovation expertise, and ideas<br>- Number of approved product, and service initiatives resulting from innovative ideas |

**Metrics**

The following section contains the enterprise goals, and IT-related goals, with sample metrics that can be used to measure the achievement of each goal. These metrics are samples, and every enterprise should carefully review the list, decide on relevant and achievable metrics for its own environment, and design its own scorecard system.

## 3.2 Enterprise goal metrics

Table 3.3 contains all enterprise goals as identified in the framework publication, with sample metrics for each.

## 3.3 IT-related goal metrics

Table 3.4 contains all IT-related goals as defined in the goals cascade, and includes sample metrics for each goal.

Table 3.4 IT-related goal sample metrics
Source: EDM01 Ensure Governance Framework Setting and Maintenance, EDM02 Ensure Benefits Delivery [– etc.],
COBIT 5: Enabling Processes, 2012 © ISACA.

| BSC Dimensions | Enterprise goals | Metrics |
|---|---|---|
| Financial | 1. Alignment of IT, and business strategy | - Percent of enterprise strategic goals, and requirements supported by IT strategic goals<br>- Stakeholder satisfaction with scope of the planned portfolio of programs, and services<br>- Percent of IT value drivers mapped to business value drivers |
| | 2. IT compliance, and support for business compliance with external laws, and regulations | - Cost of IT non-compliance, including settlements, and fines<br>- Number of IT-related non-compliance issues reported to the board or causing public comment or embarrassment<br>- Number of non-compliance issues relating to contractual agreements with IT service providers<br>- Coverage of compliance assessments |
| | 3. Commitment of executive management for making IT-related decisions | - Percent of executive management roles with clearly defined accountabilities for IT decisions<br>- Number of times IT is on the board agenda in a proactive manner<br>- Frequency of IT strategy (executive) committee meetings<br>- Rate of execution of executive IT-related decisions |

| BSC Dimensions | Enterprise goals | Metrics |
|---|---|---|
| | 4. Managed IT-related business risks | - Percent of critical business processes, IT services, and IT-enabled business programs covered by risk assessment<br>- Number of significant IT-related incidents that were not identified in risk assessment<br>- Percent of enterprise risk assessments including IT-related risks<br>- Update frequency of risk profile |
| | 5. Realized benefits from IT-enabled investments, and services portfolio | - Percent of IT-enabled investments where benefit realization monitored through full economic life cycle<br>- Percent of IT services where expected benefits realized<br>- Percent of IT-enabled investments where claimed benefits met or exceeded |
| Customer | 6. Transparency of IT costs, benefits, and risk | - Percent of investment business cases with clearly defined, and approved expected IT-related costs, and benefits<br>- Percent of IT services with clearly defined, and approved operational costs, and expected benefits<br>- Satisfaction survey of key stakeholders regarding the transparency, understanding, and accuracy of IT financial information |
| | 7. Delivery of IT services in line with business requirements | - Number of business disruptions due to IT service incidents<br>- Percent of business stakeholders satisfied that IT service delivery meets agreed-upon service levels<br>- Percent of users satisfied with quality of IT service delivery<br>- Adequate usage of applications, information, and technology solutions |
| | 8. Percent of business process owners satisfied with supporting IT products, and services | - Level of business user understanding of how technology solutions support their processes<br>- Satisfaction level of business users with training, and user manuals |
| | 9. IT agility | - Level of satisfaction of business executives with IT's responsiveness to new requirements<br>- Number of critical business processes supported by up-to-date infrastructure, and applications<br>- Average time to turn strategic IT objectives into an agreed and approved initiative |
| | 10. Security of information, and processing infrastructure, and applications | - Number of security incidents causing business disruption or public embarrassment<br>- Number of IT services with outstanding security requirements<br>- Time to grant, change, and remove access privileges, compared to agreed service levels<br>- Frequency of security assessment against latest standards, and guidelines |

| BSC Dimensions | Enterprise goals | Metrics |
|---|---|---|
| Internal | 11. Optimization of IT assets, resources, and capabilities | - Frequency of capability maturity, and cost optimization assessments<br>- Trend of assessment results<br>- Satisfaction levels of business and IT executives with IT-related costs, and capabilities |
| | 12. Enablement, and support of business processes by integrating applications, and technology into business processes | - Number of business processing incidents caused by technology integration errors<br>- Number of business process changes that need to be delayed or reworked because of technology integration issues<br>- Number of IT-enabled business programs delayed or incurring additional cost due to technology integration issues<br>- Number of applications or critical infrastructures operating in silos, and not integrated |
| | 13. Delivery of programs on time, on budget, and meeting requirements, and quality standards | - Number of programs/projects on time, and within budget<br>- Percent of stakeholders satisfied with program/project quality<br>- Number of programs needing significant rework due to quality defects<br>- Cost of application maintenance vs. overall IT cost |
| | 14. Availability of reliable and useful information | - Level of business user satisfaction with quality of management information<br>- Number of business process incidents caused by non-availability of information<br>- Ratio and extent of erroneous business decisions where erroneous or unavailable information was key factor |
| | 15. IT compliance with internal policies | - Number of incidents related to non-compliance to policy<br>- Percent of stakeholders who understand policies<br>- Percent of policies supported by effective standards, and working practices<br>- Frequency of policies review, and update<br>- Learning and Growth |
| Learning and growth | 16. Competent and motivated IT personnel | - Percent of staff whose IT-related skills are sufficient for the competency required for their role<br>- Percent of staff satisfied with their IT-related roles<br>- Number of learning/training hours per staff |
| | 17. Knowledge, expertise, and initiatives for business innovation | - Level of business executive awareness, and understanding of IT innovation possibilities<br>- Stakeholder satisfaction with levels of IT innovation expertise, and ideas<br>- Number of approved initiatives resulting from innovative IT ideas |

## 3.4 Drivers and benefits

### Drivers

The major drivers for the development of the framework include:

- A need to link together and reinforce all major ISACA research, frameworks and guidance, with a primary focus on COBIT, Val IT and Risk IT, but also considering, amongst others, BMIS, ITAF, Board Briefing on IT Governance, and Taking Governance Forward
- A need to connect to, and (where relevant) align with, other major frameworks and standards in the marketplace, such as ITIL®, The Open Group Architecture Forum (TOGAF®), Project Management Body of Knowledge (PMBOK®), PRINCE2® and the International Organization for Standardization (ISO®) standards. This will help stakeholders understand how various frameworks, best practices and standards are positioned relative to each other and how they can be used together and could augment each other.
- A need to provide further guidance in areas with high interest, such as enterprise architecture, asset and service management, and the management of IT innovation and emerging technologies
- A recognition that there are many current and potential users who wish to focus on specific topics, who find it difficult to navigate current material and identify content that will satisfy their requirements. There is also a general need to improve ease of use and ease of navigation and to bring consistency in concepts, terminology, and the level of detail provided by ISACA.
- A need to ensure that the scope covers the full end-to-end business and IT functional responsibilities, and a need to cover all aspects that lead to effective governance and management of enterprise IT, such as organizational structures, policies, culture, etc., over and above processes. This is especially important given the increasing pervasiveness of IT and it helps increase transparency.
- A need to for the enterprise to achieve increased:
  o Value creation through enterprise IT
  o Business user satisfaction with IT engagement and services
  o Compliance with relevant laws, regulations, and policies

### Benefits

COBIT 5 brings a substantial number of benefits to enterprises, improving on guidance previously available from ISACA. Table 3.5 summarizes the business benefits, the impacts that will bring about the benefits, and the fundamental capabilities delivering the benefits, and points to more information in the framework.

**Table 3.5 Benefits**

Source COBIT 5 Business Framework COBIT 5: Enabling Processes, 2012 © ISACA.

| Benefits | Impacts that will bring about these benefits | New capabilities delivering this benefit | More information on the changes |
|---|---|---|---|
| Enterprise wide benefits:<br>• Increased value creation through enterprise IT<br>• Increased business user satisfaction with IT engagement and services. IT seen as a fundamental enabler<br>• Increased compliance with relevant laws, regulations and policies<br><br>IT function has become more business-focused | Key business impacts of COBIT 5 include:<br>• Increased business focus on organizational governance and management of IT. This has become a part of the enterprise's good practices<br>• Increased transparency in decision making for the organizational governance of IT<br><br>Key IT impacts of COBIT 5 include:<br>• Increased agility of IT to respond to business needs<br>• Increased alignment of IT tasks/ activities with business need<br>• Increased optimization of IT assets and resources<br>• Optimized IT-related business risk<br>• Optimized cost performance of IT | COBIT 5 provides new capabilities for effective organizational governance and management of IT:<br>• The starting point of governance and management activities is the stakeholder needs related to enterprise IT<br>• Creates a more holistic, integrated, and complete view of organizational governance and management of IT that:<br>  ○ Is consistent<br>  ○ Provides an end-to-end view on all IT-related matters<br>  ○ Provides a systemic view<br>  ○ Creates a common language between IT and business for the organizational governance and management of IT<br>• Is consistent with generally accepted corporate governance standards, and thus helps to meet regulatory requirements<br>• Creates a clear distinction between governance and management of organizational governance of IT | Section 3 provides more information on stakeholders, their typical needs and how these can be linked to practical enabler goals in COBIT 5. This is described by means of the COBIT 5 goals cascade.<br>All good-practice advice contained in COBIT 5 is consolidated into a knowledge base, combining the strengths and experiences of the guidance, research, and frameworks of COBIT, Val IT, Risk IT, BMIS, ITAF, and the Board Briefing.<br>COBIT 5 is relevant to and aligned with the most important standards and frameworks, e.g., ISO/IEC 38500 and other recent global governmental and market-driven enterprise and governance of enterprise IT initiatives.<br>In addition, the compliance requirement is covered throughout COBIT 5, from being recognized as one of the enterprise goals to being embedded in processes and practices and other enablers.<br>In COBIT 5: Process Reference Guide, compliance is embedded in the processes and practices.<br>Introduces consistency, linkages and views with other leading frameworks and standards, e.g., generally accepted corporate governance, and standards, regulatory and compliance requirements. |

| Benefits | Impacts that will bring about these benefits | New capabilities delivering this benefit | More information on the changes |
|---|---|---|---|
| | | • Increases the content (depth and breadth) and connection to relevant contemporary governance developments <br> • Creates an integrator framework and structure for enablers (including processes) that are uniform across the enterprise for both IT and business to use <br> • COBIT 5 includes an information model (IM). <br> • Information is a crucial enabler and fundamental resource for the whole enterprise. Information is stored and processed by IT, but is generated, used and creates value by its business use. By providing a unique model – the IM – COBIT 5 connects the business areas with IT in the most efficient and effective way. | Introduces further guidance in high-interest areas for organizational governance and management of IT, e.g., enterprise architecture, emerging technologies (e.g., cloud), and innovation. <br> In Section 4 and Appendix H, COBIT 5 introduces a set of principles and enablers for the organizational governance and management of IT. <br> Enablers include processes; information; people and skills; organizational structures; culture, ethics and behavior; principles; and policies. The simple models included with COBIT for governance enablers (policies, structures, processes, etc.) are not specific for IT. They can be used to govern and manage business areas as well, thus providing a uniform way of dealing with all processes in the enterprise. <br> COBIT 5 has integrated – in its enabler model – all IT-related activities an enterprise should undertake, including core IT processes and activities, but also all activities required from business stakeholders. Section 5 describes the overall enabler model. |

# CHAPTER 4

# Detailed description of the enabler models

## 4.1 Overview of this section

The specific diagram for each enabler contains a number of additional components. Each diagram is accompanied by a list of specific components and relationships with other enablers.

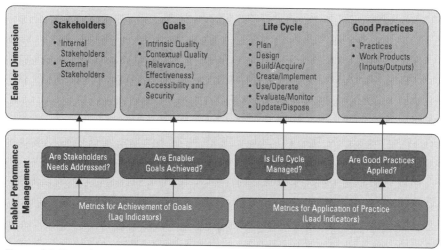

Figure 4.1  Generic enabler model

Source Figure 13, COBIT 5 Enablers: Generic,COBIT 5: A Business Framework for the Governance and Management of Enterprise IT, 2012 © ISACA.

## 4.2   Process model

Figure 4.2 shows at a high level the different components of a process as it is defined within the framework. A process is defined as "a collection of activities that takes one or more kinds of input and creates an output that is of value to the enterprise".

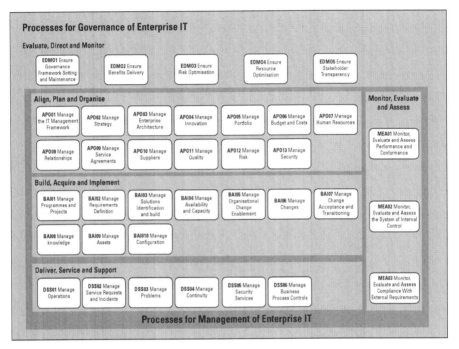

**Figure 4.2  Process model**

Source Figure 16, COBIT 5 Process Reference Model, COBIT 5: A Business Framework for the Governance and Management of Enterprise IT, 2012 © ISACA.

The process model shows:
- Stakeholders
- Goals and metrics
- Lifecycle
- Generic process practices
- Good practices[23]
    - o Practices
    - o Activities

---

23 Only practices and activities are developed under the current project. The more detailed level(s) are subject to additional development(s), e.g., the various practitioner guides may provide more detailed guidance for their area.

- Attributes
    - Inputs and outputs[24]
    - Process capability level
    - RACI chart
- Relationships with other enablers

## 4.3 Information model

The information model (IM) is an extension of the generic enabler model; it defines a number of specific dimensions of information, allowing all stakeholders who have to deal with information to consider all required aspects. The information model deals with all information relevant for enterprises, not only automated information. Information can be structured or "non-structured" or not formalized. One can think of Information as being one stage in the "information cycle" of an enterprise. In the information cycle (Figure 4.3), business processes generate and process data, transforming it to information and knowledge, and ultimately generating value for the enterprise. The scope of the IM excludes the knowledge and value parts of the cycle.

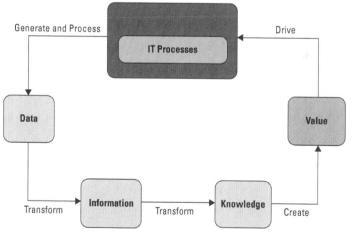

Figure 4.3 Metadata: information cycle
Source Figure 35, COBIT 5 Metadata - Information Cycle, COBIT 5: A Business Framework for the Governance and Management of Enterprise IT, 2012 © ISACA.

---

24 The illustrative COBIT 5 inputs and outputs should not be regarded as an exhaustive list since additional information flows could be defined depending on a particular organisation's environment and process framework.

Figure 4.4 shows all components of the information model, with the specific components highlighted in Bold typeface.

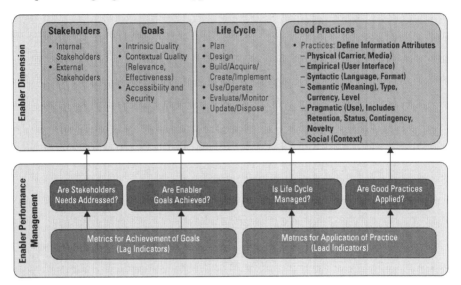

Figure 4.4 Information model

Source Figure 36, COBIT 5 Enabler Information,COBIT 5: A Business Framework for the Governance and Management of Enterprise IT, 2012 © ISACA.

Information stakeholders can be internal or external to the enterprise. In addition, their stakes need to be identified. With respect to which information stakeholders exist, different categorizations of roles in dealing with information are possible:

- Information producer, responsible for creating the information
- Information custodian, responsible for storing and maintaining the information
- Information consumer, responsible for using the information

**Information quality**

**Quality Goals**
- Intrinsic quality
  - ○ Accuracy
  - ○ Objectivity
  - ○ Believability
  - ○ Reputation

- Contextual and representational quality
  - Relevancy
  - Completeness
  - Timeliness
  - Appropriate amount of information
  - Concise representation
  - Consistent representation
  - Interpretability
  - Understandability
  - Ease of manipulation
- Accessibility quality
  - Availability
  - Confidentiality

## Information economical goals

- Information lifecycle
  - Plan
  - Obtain
  - Store
  - Share
  - Use
  - Dispose
- Information attributes
  - Physical world layer
  - Empiric layer
  - Syntactic layer
  - Semantic layer
    - Information type
    - Information currency
    - Information level
  - Pragmatic layer
    - Retention period
    - Information status
    - Novelty
    - Contingency
  - Social world layer
    - Context

## 4.4   Organizational structures model

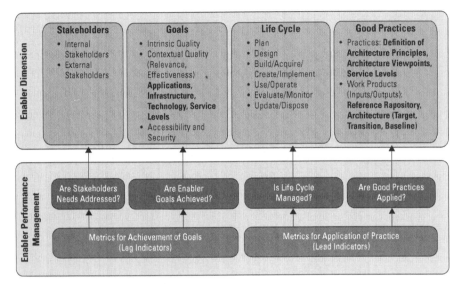

Figure 4.5 Organizational structures model
Source Figure 37, COBIT 5 Enabler: Services, Infrastructure and Applications,COBIT 5: A Business Framework for the Governance and Management of Enterprise IT, 2012 © ISACA.

The organizational structures model shows:
- Stakeholders
- Goals and metrics
- Lifecycle
- Good practices
  - o Operating principles
  - o Delegation of authority
  - o Escalation procedures
- Attributes
  - o Composition
  - o Inputs and outputs
  - o RACI chart
  - o Span of control
  - o Level of authority/decision rights
- Relationships with other enablers
  - o Culture and behavior
  - o Composition of organizational structures
  - o The mandate and operating principles
  - o Relationships with other processes

The following illustrative process reference model includes RACI charts, which use a number of roles and structures. Table 4.1 describes these predefined roles and structures.

## Table 4.1 Roles and organizational structures

Source Figure 33, COBIT 5 Roles and Organisational Structures, COBIT 5: A Business Framework for the Governance and Management of Enterprise IT, 2012 © ISACA.

| Role/structure | Definition/description |
|---|---|
| Board | The group of the most senior executives and/or non-executives of the enterprise who are accountable for the governance of the enterprise and have overall control of its resources |
| Chief executive officer (CEO) | The highest-ranking officer who is in charge of the total management of the enterprise |
| Chief financial officer (CFO) | The most senior official of the enterprise who is accountable for all aspects of financial management including financial risk and controls and reliable and accurate accounts |
| Chief operating officer (COO) | The most senior official of the enterprise who is accountable for the operation of the enterprise |
| Chief risk officer (CRO) | The most senior official of the enterprise who is accountable for all aspects of risk management across the enterprise. An IT risk officer function may be established to oversee IT-related risk. |
| Chief information officer (CIO) | The most senior official of the enterprise who is responsible for aligning IT and business strategies and accountable for planning, resourcing and managing the delivery of IT services and solutions to support enterprise objectives |
| Chief information security officer (CISO) | The most senior official of the enterprise who is accountable for the security of enterprise information in all its forms |
| Business executive | A senior management individual accountable for the operation of a specific business unit or subsidiary |
| Business process owner | An individual accountable for the performance of a process in realizing its objectives, driving process improvement, and approving process changes |
| Strategy (IT executive) committee | A group of senior executives appointed by the board to ensure that the board is involved in and kept informed of major IT-related matters and decisions. The committee is accountable for managing the portfolios of IT-enabled investments, IT services, and IT assets, ensuring that value is delivered and risks are managed. The committee is normally chaired by a board member, not the CIO |
| (Project and program) steering committees | A group of stakeholders and experts who are accountable for guidance of programs and projects, including management and monitoring of plans, allocation of resources, delivery of benefits and value, and management of program and project risks |
| Architecture board | A group of stakeholders and experts who are accountable for guidance on enterprise architecture-related matters and decisions, and for setting architectural policies and standards |

| Role/structure | Definition/description |
|---|---|
| Enterprise risk committee | The group of executives of the enterprise who are accountable for the enterprise-level collaboration and consensus required to support enterprise risk management activities and decisions. An IT risk council may be established to consider IT risk in more detail and advise the Enterprise Risk Committee. |
| Head human resources | The most senior official of an enterprise who is accountable for planning and policies with respect to all human resources in that enterprise |
| Compliance | The function in the enterprise responsible for guidance on legal, regulatory and contractual compliance |
| Audit | The function in the enterprise responsible for provision of internal and external audits |
| Head architect | A senior individual accountable for the enterprise architecture process |
| Head development | A senior individual accountable for IT-related solution development processes |
| Head IT operations | A senior individual accountable for the IT operational environments and infrastructure |
| Head IT administration | A senior individual accountable for IT-related records and responsible for supporting IT related administrative matters |
| Program and project management office (PMO) | The function responsible for supporting program and project managers, and gathering, assessing and reporting information about the conduct of their programs and constituent projects |
| Value management office (VMO) | The function that acts as the secretariat for managing investment and service portfolios, including assessing and advising on investment opportunities and business cases, recommending value governance/management methods and controls, and reporting on progress on sustaining and creating value from investments and services |
| Service manager | An individual who manages the development, implementation, evaluation and on-going management of new and existing products and services for a specific customer (user) or group of customers (users) |
| Information security manager | An individual who manages, designs, oversees and/or assesses an enterprise's information security |
| Business continuity manager | An individual who manages, designs, oversees and/or assesses an enterprise's business continuity capability, to ensure that the enterprise's critical functions continue to operate following disruptive events |
| Privacy officer | An individual who is responsible for monitoring the risks and business impacts of privacy laws and for guiding and coordinating the implementation of policies and activities that will ensure that the privacy directives are met |

## 4.5  Skills and competencies model

The people and skills model is shown in Figure 4.6. The purpose of this model is to provide the necessary components to provide guidance on how people skills and behavior can be influenced and structured.

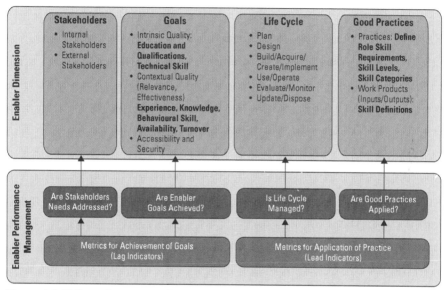

Figure 4.6  Skills and competencies model

Source Figure 38, COBIT 5 Enabler: People, Skills and Competencies,COBIT 5: A Business Framework for the Governance and Management of Enterprise IT, 2012 © ISACA.

The Skills and Competencies model shows:
- Stakeholders
- Goals and metrics
- Lifecycle:
- Good practices:
  - Internal good practice
  - External good practice
- Attributes
- Relationships with other processes

Table 4.2 Skills categories

Source Figures 15 and 16,COBIT 5: A Business Framework for the Governance and Management of Enterprise IT, 2012 © ISACA.

| Process domain | Examples of skill categories |
|---|---|
| Evaluate, direct and monitor | - Governance of enterprise IT |
| Align, plan and organize | - IT policy formulation<br>- IT strategy<br>- Enterprise architecture<br>- Innovation<br>- Financial management<br>- Portfolio management |
| Build, acquire and implement | - Business analysis<br>- Project management<br>- Usability evaluation<br>- Requirements definition and management<br>- Programming<br>- System ergonomics<br>- Software decommissioning |
| Deliver, service and support | - Capacity management<br>- Availability management<br>- Problem management<br>- Service desk and incident management<br>- Security administration<br>- IT operations<br>- Database administration |
| Monitor, evaluate and assess | - Compliance review<br>- Performance monitoring<br>- Controls audit |

## 4.6   Principles and policies model

The principles and policies model is shown in Figure 4.7.

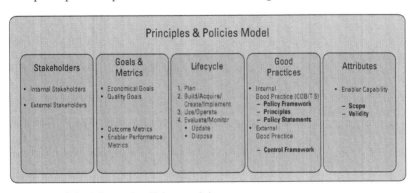

Figure 4.7  Principles and policies model

Source Figure 34, COBIT 5 Enabler: Culture, Ethics,COBIT 5: A Business Framework for the Governance and Management of Enterprise IT, 2012 © ISACA.

The principles and policies model shows:
- Stakeholders
- Goals and metrics
- Principles need to be:
  o Limited in number
  o Put in simple language
- Good policies are
  o Effective
  o Efficient
  o Non-intrusive
- Lifecycle – points to be taken into account include:
  o Access to policies
- Currency of policies
- Good practices
- Attributes
- Relationships with other processes

## 4.7 Culture, ethics, and behavior model[25]

Human behavior is one of the key factors determining the success of any enterprise, and the model for culture, ethics, and behavior provides a number of components that need to be taken into account.

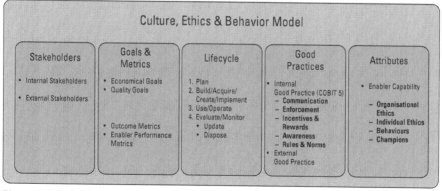

Figure 4.8 Culture, ethics, and behavior model

25 Source material COBIT 5 Enabler: Services, Infrastructure and Applications, COBIT 5: A Business Framework for the Governance and Management of Enterprise IT, 2012 © ISACA.

The culture, ethics, and behavior model shows:
- Stakeholders
- Goals and metrics
- Lifecycle
- Good practices
  o Communication
  o Awareness
  o Incentives
  o Rules and norms
- Attributes
  o Organizational ethics
  o Individual ethics
  o Behaviors
  o Behavior toward taking risk
  o Behavior toward following policy
- Relationships with other processes

## 4.8   Service capabilities model

Service capabilities refer to resources such as applications and infrastructures that are leveraged in the delivery of IT-related services.

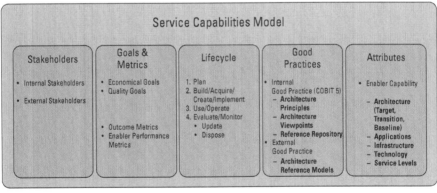

Figure 4.9  Service capabilities model

The service capabilities model shows:
- Stakeholders
- Goals and metrics

- Lifecycle
- Good practices
  - Definition of architecture principles
    - Re-use
    - Buy vs. build
    - Simplicity
    - Agility
    - Openness
  - The enterprise's models, catalogues, and matrices
  - An architecture management information system
  - Technical Reference Model
  - Integrated Information Infrastructure Reference Model (e.g. TOGAF[26])
  - ITIL provides comprehensive guidance on how to design and operate services.
    - Service attributes
    - Service resources
- Cultural and behavioral aspects
- Relationships with other processes
- Relationships with other enablers

---

# CHAPTER 5

# The process model

## 5.1 The process model

A process is defined as "a collection of activities that takes one or more kinds of input, and creates an output that is of value to the enterprise".

Figure 5.1 shows at a high level the different components of a process as it is defined within COBIT 5.

The process model shows:

**1. Stakeholders**
Processes have internal and external stakeholders, each with their own roles. Stakeholders and their responsibility levels are documented in RACI charts, which are an attribute of the process.

**2. Goals and metrics**
Process goals are defined as "a statement describing the desired outcome of a process. An outcome can be an artifact, a significant change of a state or a significant capability improvement of other processes'. At each level, metrics are defined to measure the extent to which these goals are achieved. Metrics can be defined as *"a quantifiable entity that allows the measurement of the achievement of a process goal. Metrics should be specific, measurable, actionable, relevant, and timely (SMART)"*.

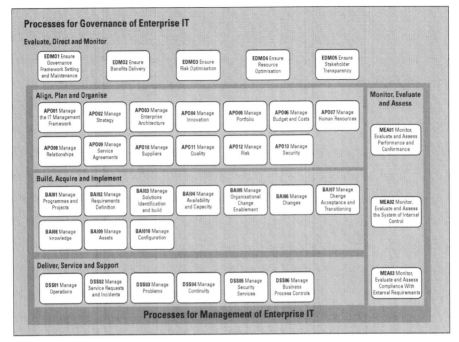

Figure 5.1 The process model revisited
Source Figure 16, COBIT 5 Process Reference Model, COBIT 5: A Business Framework for the Governance and Management of Enterprise IT, 2012 © ISACA.

## 3. Life cycle

Each process has a lifecycle, i.e., it is defined, created, operated, monitored, and adjusted/updated or retired. Generic process practices, such as those defined in the COBIT process assessment model, based on ISO/IEC 15504, can assist with defining, running, monitoring, and optimizing processes.

## 4. Good practices

Process internal good practices are described in cascading levels of detail, i.e., practices, activities, and detailed activities.[27]

*Practices:*

- For each COBIT process, the management practices provide a complete set of high-level requirements for effective and practical management (governance) of enterprise IT. They:

---

27 Only practices and activities are developed under the current COBIT 5 project. The more detailed level(s) are subject to additional development(s), e.g., the various practitioner guides may provide more detailed guidance for their area

- o Are statements of managerial actions to increase value, reduce risk, and manage resources
- o Are aligned with relevant generally accepted standards, and best practices
- o Are generic, and applicable for any enterprise
- o Cover business and IT role players in the process (end to end)
- Enterprise management needs to make choices relative to these management practices/governance practices by:
  - o Selecting those that are applicable
  - o Deciding upon those that will be implemented
  - o Choosing how to implement them (frequency, span, automation, etc.)
  - o Accepting the risk of not implementing those that may apply

*Activities*

Activities are defined as *"guidance to achieve key management practices for successful governance, and management of enterprise IT"*. This is of use to:
- Management, service providers, end-users, and IT professionals who need to justify, and design or improve specific practices
- Assurance professionals who may be asked for their opinions regarding proposed implementations or necessary improvements

The activities:
- Describe a set of necessary and sufficient action-oriented implementation steps to achieve a management practice/governance practice
- Consider the inputs, and outputs of the process
- Are based on generally accepted standards, and best practices
- Support establishment of clear roles, and responsibilities
- Are non-prescriptive, and need to be adapted, and developed into specific procedures appropriate for the enterprise

*Detailed activities*

Activities may not be at a sufficient level of detail for implementation, and further guidance may need to be:
- Obtained from specific relevant standards, and best practices such as ITIL, the ISO/IEC 27000 series, and PRINCE2
- Developed as more detailed or specific activities in the framework itself

External good practices can exist in any form or level of detail, and mostly refer to other standards and frameworks. Users can refer to these external good practice at all times, knowing that the framework is aligned with these standards where relevant, and mapping information will be made available. Successful completion of process activities, and delivery of work products are the process performance indicators for process capability achievement.

## 5. Attributes

There is a number of specific process attributes defined in the framework process model. These include:

- Inputs and outputs – The inputs and outputs are the process work products/ artifacts considered necessary to support operation of the process. They enable key decisions, provide a record, and audit trail of process activities, and enable follow-up in the event of an incident. They are defined at the key governance/ management practice level, may include some work products used only within the process, and are often essential inputs to other processes.[28]
- Process capability level – the framework includes an ISO/IEC 15504V-based process capability assessment scheme. The result of such an assessment is an attribute of a process
- RACI chart, as described earlier

## 6. Relationships with other enablers

There are multiple relationships with other enablers, e.g.:

- Processes need information (as one of the types of inputs), and can produce information (as a work product)
- Processes need organizational structures, and roles to operate, which are expressed through the RACI charts, e.g., IT steering committee/group, enterprise risk committee, board, audit, CIO, CEO
- Processes generate service capabilities (management, enterprise, processes, knowledge, and people)
- Processes depend on other processes
- Processes require policies and procedures to ensure consistent implementation and execution
- Cultural and behavioral aspects determine how well processes are executed
- Processes require the skills and competencies of individuals to support effective performance and deliver quality outcomes

---

28 The illustrative COBIT 5 inputs, and outputs should not be regarded as an exhaustive list since additional information flows could be defined depending on a particular enterprise's environment, and process framework

## 5.2  Governance and management processes

One of the guiding principles is the distinction made between governance and management. When considering processes for governance, and management in the context of the enterprise, the difference between types of processes lies into the objectives of the processes:

- Governance processes deal with the governance objectives – value delivery, risk management, and resource balancing, and include practices, and activities aimed at evaluating strategic options, providing direction to IT, and monitoring the outcome.
- In line with the definition of management, practices and activities management processes cover the responsibility areas of Plan, Build, Run, and Monitor (PBRM) enterprise IT, and they provide end-to-end coverage of IT. Although the outcome of both types of processes is different, and intended for a different audience, internally, i.e., from the context of the process itself, all processes require "planning", "building or implementation", "execution", and "monitoring" activities.

## 5.3  Process reference model

COBIT 5 is not prescriptive, but it advocates that enterprises implement governance and management processes such that the key areas are covered, as shown in Figure 5.2.

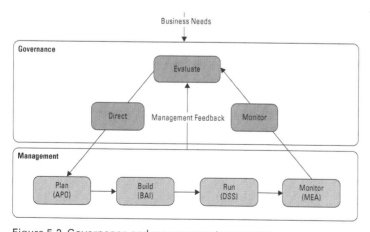

Figure 5.2  Governance and management processes

Source Figure 15, COBIT 5 Governance and Management Key Areas, COBIT 5: A Business Framework for the Governance and Management of Enterprise IT, 2012 © ISACA.

The process reference model defines and describes in detail a number of governance and management processes. It represents all the processes normally found in an enterprise relating to IT activities, thus providing a common reference model understandable to operational IT, and business managers, and their auditors/ advisors. The process reference model divides the processes of enterprise IT into two domains – governance, and management:

The **governance** domain contains five governance processes; within each process, evaluate, direct, and monitor practices are defined:
- EDM01 Ensure governance framework setting and maintenance
- EDM02 Ensure benefits delivery
- EDM03 Ensure risk optimization
- EDM04 Ensure resource optimization
- EDM05 Ensure stakeholder transparency

The four **management** domains, in line with the responsibility areas of Plan, Build, Run, and Monitor (PBRM) provide end-to-end coverage of IT:
- Align, Plan and organize
- Build, acquire and implement
- Deliver, service and support
- Monitor, evaluate and assess

Figure 5.3 shows the complete set of 36 governance and management processes within the framework.

Each domain contains a number of processes with most of the processes requiring "planning", "implementation", "execution", and "monitoring" activities within the process itself or within the specific issue with which it is dealing (e.g., quality, security).
- The processes are placed in domains in line with what is generally the most relevant area of activity when looking at IT at the enterprise level
- The processes also cover the full scope of business, and IT activities related to the governance, and management of enterprise IT, thus making the process model truly enterprise-wide.

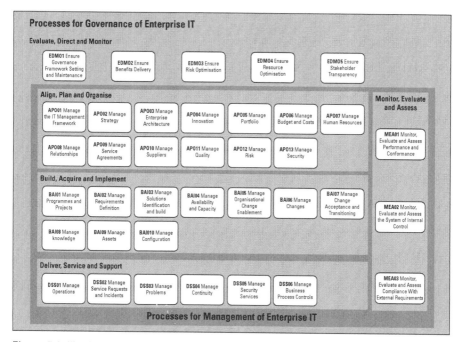

Figure 5.3 Illustrative governance and management processes

Source Figure 16, COBIT 5 Process Reference Model,COBIT 5: A Business Framework for the Governance and Management of Enterprise IT, 2012 © ISACA.

## 5.4 Process reference guide

This section contains the detailed process-related information for the COBIT 5 governance, and management processes. For each process the following information is included, in line with the process model explained in the previous section:

- Process identification – On the first page of each process description, the following information is identified:
  - Process label, consisting of the domain prefix (EDM, APO, BAI, DSS, and MEA), and the process number
  - Process name – a short description, indicating the main subject of the process
  - Area of the process – governance or management
  - Domain name

- Process description – Describes the process in more detail. A short paragraph, containing an:
  - Overview of what the process does, i.e., the purpose of the process
  - Overview at a very high level of how the process accomplishes the purpose
- Process purpose statement – describes the overall purpose of the process in a short paragraph
- Goals cascade information – Reference and description of the IT-related goals that are primarily supported by the process, and metrics to measure the achievement of the IT-related goals
- Process goals and metrics – A set of process goals and a limited number of example metrics
- RACI chart, containing a suggested assignment of level of responsibility for process practices to different roles, and structures. The different levels of involvement are represented by the characters

  **R**esponsible
  - Who is getting the task done? This refers to the roles taking the main operational stake in fulfilling the activity listed and creating the intended outcome

  **A**ccountable
  - Who accounts for the success of the task? This assigns the overall accountability for getting the task done (Where does the buck stop?). Note that the role mentioned is the lowest appropriate level of accountability; there are, of course, higher levels that are accountable, too. To enable empowerment of the enterprise, accountability is broken down as far as possible. Accountability does not indicate that the role has no operational activities; it is very likely that the role gets involved in the task. As a principle, accountability cannot be shared.

  **C**onsulted
  - Who is providing input? These are key roles that provide input. Note that it is up to the accountable and responsible role(s) to obtain information from other units or external partners, too. However, inputs from the roles listed are to be considered and, if required, appropriate action has to be taken for escalation, including the information of the process owner and/or the steering committee.

Informed
- o Who is receiving information? These are roles who are informed of the achievements and/or deliverables of the task. The role in 'accountable', of course, should always receive appropriate information to oversee the task, as does the responsible roles for their area of interest.

- Detailed description of the process practices, containing for each practice:
  - o Practice title, and description
  - o Practice inputs, and outputs, with indication of origin, and destination
  - o Process activities

Related guidance—References to other standards and direction to additional guidance

The process reference model divides the governance and management processes of enterprise IT into two main process domains – governance and management.

## 5.5 Governance Domain: Evaluate, Direct, & Monitor

- EDM01 Ensure governance framework setting and maintenance
- EDM02 Ensure benefits delivery
- EDM03 Ensure risk optimization
- EDM04 Ensure resource optimization
- EDM05 Ensure stakeholder transparency

## EDM01: Ensure governance framework setting and maintenance

| EDM01 | Ensure governance framework setting and maintenance | Domain: | Governance |
|---|---|---|---|
| | | Area: | Evaluate, Direct, & Monitor |

**Process Description**

Analyze and articulate the requirements for the governance of enterprise IT, and put in place, and maintain effective enabling structures, principles, processes, and practices, with clarity of responsibilities, and authority to achieve the enterprise's mission, goals, and objectives

**Process Purpose Statement**

Provide a consistent approach integrated and aligned with the enterprise governance approach. To ensure that IT-related decisions are made in line with the enterprise's strategies and objectives, ensure that IT processes are overseen effectively and transparently compliance with legal and regulatory requirements is confirmed, and the governance requirements for board members are met.

**The process supports the achievement of a set of IT-related goals, which support the achievement of a set of enterprise goals:**

| Ref | IT-related Goal |
|---|---|
| 01 | Alignment of IT and business strategy |
| 03 | Commitment of executive management for making IT-related decisions |
| 07 | Delivery of IT services in line with business requirements |

## EDM02: Ensure benefits delivery

| EDM02 | Ensure benefits delivery | Domain: | Governance |
|---|---|---|---|
| | | Area: | Evaluate, Direct, & Monitor |

**Process Description**

Optimize the value contribution to the business from the business processes, IT services, and IT assets resulting from investments made by IT at acceptable costs.

**Process Purpose Statement**

Secure optimal value from IT-enabled initiatives services, and assets, cost-efficient delivery of solutions, and services, and a reliable and accurate picture of costs, and likely benefits so that business needs are supported effectively, and efficiently

**The process supports the achievement of a set of IT-related goals, which support the achievement of a set of enterprise goals:**

| Ref | IT-related Goal |
|---|---|
| 01 | Alignment of IT, and business strategy |
| 05 | Realized benefits from IT-enabled investments, and services portfolio |
| 06 | Transparency of IT costs, benefits, and risk |
| 07 | Delivery of IT services in line with business requirements |
| 17 | Knowledge, expertise, and initiatives for business innovation |

## EDM03: Ensure Risk Optimization

| EDM03 | Ensure Risk Optimization | Domain: | Governance |
|---|---|---|---|
| | | Area: | Evaluate, Direct, & Monitor |

**Process Description**

Ensure that the enterprise's risk appetite and tolerance are understood, articulated, and communicated, and that risk to enterprise value related to the use of IT is identified and managed

**Process Purpose Statement**

Ensure that IT-related enterprise risk does not exceed risk appetite and risk tolerance, the impact of IT risk to enterprise value is identified and managed, and the potential for compliance failures is minimized

**The process supports the achievement of a set of IT-related goals, which support the achievement of a set of enterprise goals:**

| Ref | IT-related Goal |
|---|---|
| 04 | Managed IT-related business risks |
| 06 | Transparency of IT costs, benefits, and risk |
| 15 | IT compliance with internal policies |

## EDM04: Ensure Resource Optimization

| EDM04 | Ensure Resource Optimization | Domain: | Governance |
|---|---|---|---|
| | | Area: | Evaluate, Direct, & Monitor |

**Process Description**

Ensure that adequate and sufficient IT-related capabilities (people, process, and technology) are available to support enterprise objectives effectively at optimal cost

**Process Purpose Statement**

Ensure that the resource needs of the enterprise are met in the most optimal manner, IT costs are optimized, and there is an increased likelihood of benefit realization and readiness for future change

**The process supports the achievement of a set of IT-related goals, which support the achievement of a set of enterprise goals:**

| Ref | IT-related Goal |
|---|---|
| 09 | IT agility |
| 11 | Optimization of IT assets, resources, and capabilities |
| 16 | Competent, and motivated IT personnel |

## EDM05: Ensure Stakeholder Transparency

| EDM05 | Ensure Stakeholder Transparency | Domain: | Governance |
|-------|--------------------------------|---------|-----------|
|       |                                | Area:   | Evaluate, Direct, & Monitor |

**Process Description**

Ensure that enterprise IT performance and conformance measurement and reporting are transparent, with stakeholders approving the goals and metrics and the necessary remedial actions.

**Process Purpose Statement**

Make sure that the communication to stakeholders is effective and timely, and the basis for reporting is established to increase performance, identify areas for improvement, and confirm that IT-related objectives and strategies are in line with the enterprise's strategy

**The process supports the achievement of a set of IT-related goals, which support the achievement of a set of enterprise goals:**

| Ref | IT-related Goal |
|-----|-----------------|
| 03 | Commitment of executive management for making IT-related decisions |
| 06 | Transparency of IT costs, benefits, and risk |
| 07 | Delivery of IT services in line with business requirements |

# 5.6  Management Domain: Align, Plan, & Organize

- APO01 Manage the IT management framework
- APO02 Manage strategy
- APO03 Manage enterprise architecture
- APO04 Manage innovation
- APO05 Manage portfolio
- APO06 Manage budget and costs
- APO07 Manage human resources
- APO08 Manage relationships
- APO09 Manage service agreements
- APO10 Manage suppliers
- APO11 Manage quality
- APO12 Manage risk
- APO13 Manage security

## APO01: Manage the IT management framework

| APO01 | Manage the IT management framework | Domain: | Management |
|---|---|---|---|
| | | Area: | Align, Plan, & Organize |

**Process Description**

Clarify and maintain the governance of enterprise IT mission and vision. Implement and maintain mechanisms and authorities to manage information and the use of IT in the enterprise in support of governance objectives are in line with guiding principles and policies.

**Process Purpose Statement**

Provide a consistent management approach to enable the enterprise governance requirements to be met, covering management processes, organizational structures, roles, and responsibilities, reliable and repeatable activities, skills and competencies

**The process supports the achievement of a set of IT-related goals, which support the achievement of a set of enterprise goals:**

| Ref | IT-related Goal |
|---|---|
| 01 | Alignment of IT and business strategy |
| 02 | IT compliance and support for business compliance with external laws and regulations |
| 09 | IT agility |
| 11 | Optimization of IT assets, resources, and capabilities |
| 15 | IT compliance with internal policies |
| 16 | Competent and motivated IT personnel |
| 17 | Knowledge, expertise, and initiatives for business innovation |

## APO02: Manage strategy

| APO02 | Manage strategy | Domain: | Management |
|---|---|---|---|
| | | Area: | Align, Plan, & Organize |

**Process Description**

Provide a holistic view of the current business and IT environment, the future direction, and the initiatives required to migrate to the desired future environment. Leverage enterprise architecture building blocks and components, including externally provided services and related capabilities to enable nimble, reliable and efficient response to strategic objectives

**Process Purpose Statement**

Align strategic IT plans with business objectives. Clearly communicate the objectives and associated accountabilities so they are understood by all with the IT strategic options identified, structured and integrated with the business plans.

**The process supports the achievement of a set of IT-related goals, which support the achievement of a set of enterprise goals:**

| Ref | IT-related Goal |
|---|---|
| 01 | Alignment of IT and business strategy |
| 07 | Delivery of IT services in line with business requirements |
| 17 | Knowledge, expertise, and initiatives for business innovation |

## APO03: Manage Enterprise Architecture

| APO03 | Manage Enterprise Architecture | Domain: | Management |
|---|---|---|---|
| | | Area: | Align, Plan, & Organize |

**Process Description**

Establish a common architecture consisting of business process, information, and data, application, and technology architecture layers for effectively and efficiently realizing enterprise and IT strategies by creating key models and practices that describe the baseline and target architectures. Define requirements for taxonomy, standards, guidelines, procedures, templates and tools, and provide a linkage for these components. Improve alignment, increase agility, improve quality of information and generate potential cost savings through initiatives such as re-use of building block components

**Process Purpose Statement**

Represent the different building blocks that make up the enterprise and their inter-relationships as well as the principles guiding their design and evolution over time, enabling a standard, responsive, and efficient delivery of operational and strategic objectives

**The process supports the achievement of a set of IT-related goals, which support the achievement of a set of enterprise goals:**

| Ref | IT-related Goal |
|---|---|
| 01 | Alignment of IT and business strategy |
| 09 | IT agility |
| 11 | Optimization of IT assets, resources, and capabilities |

## APO04: Manage Innovation

| APO04 | Manage Innovation | Domain: | Management |
|---|---|---|---|
| | | Area: | Align, Plan, & Organize |

**Process Description**

Maintain an awareness of information technology and related service trends, identify innovation opportunities, and plan how to benefit from innovation in relation to business needs. Analyze what opportunities for business innovation or improvement can be created by emerging technologies, services, or IT-enabled business innovation, as well as through existing established technologies and by business and IT process innovation. Influence strategic planning and enterprise architecture decisions.

**Process Purpose Statement**

Achieve competitive advantage, business innovation, and improved operational effectiveness and efficiency by exploiting information technology developments.

**The process supports the achievement of a set of IT-related goals, which support the achievement of a set of enterprise goals:**

| Ref | IT-related Goal |
|---|---|
| 05 | Realized benefits from IT-enabled investments and services portfolio |
| 08 | Adequate usage of applications, information, and technology solutions |
| 09 | IT agility |
| 11 | Optimization of IT assets, resources, and capabilities |
| 17 | Knowledge, expertise and initiatives for business innovation |

## APO05: Manage Portfolio

| APO05 Manage Portfolio | Domain: | Management |
|---|---|---|
| | Area: | Align, Plan, & Organize |

**Process Description**

Execute the strategic direction set for investments in line with the enterprise architecture vision and the desired characteristics of the investment and related services portfolios, and consider the different categories of investments and the resources and funding constraints. Evaluate, prioritize, and balance programs and services, managing demand within resources, and funding constraints, based on their alignment with strategic objectives enterprise worth and risk. Move selected programs into the active services portfolio for execution. Monitor the performance of the overall portfolio of services and programs, proposing adjustments as necessary in response to program and service performance or changing enterprise priorities.

**Process Purpose Statement**

Optimize the performance of the overall portfolio of programs in response to programme and service performance and changing enterprise priorities and demands

**The process supports the achievement of a set of IT-related goals, which support the achievement of a set of enterprise goals:**

| Ref | IT-related Goal |
|---|---|
| 01 | Alignment of IT and business strategy |
| 05 | Realized benefits from IT-enabled investments, and services portfolio |
| 13 | Delivery of programs on time, on budget, and meeting requirements and quality standards |

## APO06: Manage Budget, and Costs

| APO06 Manage Budget, and Costs | Domain: | Management |
|---|---|---|
| | Area: | Align, Plan, & Organize |

**Process Description**

Manage the IT-related financial activities in the business and IT functions, covering budget, cost and benefit management, and prioritization of spending through the use of formal budgeting practices and a fair and equitable system of allocating costs to the enterprise. Consult stakeholders to identify and control the total costs and benefits within the context of the IT strategic and tactical plans, and initiate corrective action where needed.

**Process Purpose Statement**

Foster partnership between IT and enterprise stakeholders to enable the effective and efficient use of IT-related resources and provide transparency and accountability of the cost and business value of solutions and services. Enable the enterprise to make informed decisions regarding the use of IT solutions and services

**The process supports the achievement of a set of IT-related goals, which support the achievement of a set of enterprise goals:**

| Ref | IT-related Goal |
|---|---|
| 05 | Realized benefits from IT-enabled investments, and services portfolio |
| 06 | Transparency of IT costs, benefits, and risk |

## APO07: Manage Human Resources

| APO07 | Manage Human Resources | Domain: | Management |
|---|---|---|---|
| | | Area: | Align, Plan, & Organize |

**Process Description**

Provide a structured approach to ensure optimal structuring, placement, decision rights, and skills of human resources. This includes communicating the defined roles and responsibilities, learning and growth plans, and performance expectations, supported with competent and motivated people

**Process Purpose Statement**

Optimize the human resource capabilities to meet enterprise objectives

**The process supports the achievement of a set of IT-related goals, which support the achievement of a set of enterprise goals:**

| Ref | IT-related Goal |
|---|---|
| 01 | Alignment of IT and business strategy |
| 11 | Optimization of IT assets, resources, and capabilities |
| 13 | Delivery of programs on time, on budget, and meeting requirements and quality standards |
| 16 | Competent and motivated IT personnel |
| 17 | Knowledge, expertise and initiatives for business innovation |

## APO08: Manage Relationships

| APO08 | Manage Relationships | Domain: | Management |
|---|---|---|---|
| | | Area: | Align, Plan, & Organize |

**Process Description**

Manage the relationship between the business and IT in a formalized and transparent way that ensures a focus on achieving a common and shared goal of successful enterprise outcomes in support of strategic goals and within the constraint of budgets and risk tolerance. Base the relationship on mutual trust, using open and understandable terms and common language and a willingness to take ownership and accountability for key decisions.

**Process Purpose Statement**

Create improved outcomes, increased confidence, trust in IT, and effective use of resources

**The process supports the achievement of a set of IT-related goals, which support the achievement of a set of enterprise goals:**

| Ref | IT-related Goal |
|---|---|
| 01 | Alignment of IT and business strategy |
| 07 | Delivery of IT services in line with business requirements |
| 12 | Enablement and support of business processes by integrating applications and technology into business processes |
| 17 | Knowledge, expertise and initiatives for business innovation |

## APO09: Manage Service Agreements

| APO09 | Manage Service Agreements | Domain: | Management |
|---|---|---|---|
| | | Area: | Align, Plan, & Organize |

**Process Description**

Align IT-enabled services and service levels with enterprise needs and expectations, including identification, specification, design, publishing, agreement, and monitoring of IT services, service levels and performance indicators.

**Process Purpose Statement**

Ensure that IT services and service levels meet current and future enterprise needs

**The process supports the achievement of a set of IT-related goals, which support the achievement of a set of enterprise goals:**

| Ref | IT-related Goal |
|---|---|
| 07 | Delivery of IT services in line with business requirements |
| 14 | Availability of reliable and useful information for decision making |

## APO10: Manage Suppliers

| APO10 | Manage Suppliers | Domain: | Management |
|---|---|---|---|
| | | Area: | Align, Plan, & Organize |

**Process Description**

Manage IT-related services provided by all types of suppliers to meet enterprise requirements, including the selection of suppliers, management of relationships, management of contracts, and reviewing and monitoring of supplier performance for effectiveness and compliance.

**Process Purpose Statement**

Minimize the risks associated with non-performing suppliers and ensure competitive pricing

**The process supports the achievement of a set of IT-related goals, which support the achievement of a set of enterprise goals:**

| Ref | IT-related Goal |
|---|---|
| 04 | Managed IT-related business risks |
| 07 | Delivery of IT services in line with business requirements |
| 09 | IT agility |

## APO11: Manage Quality

| APO11 | Manage Quality | Domain: | Management |
|---|---|---|---|
| | | Area: | Align, Plan, & Organize |

**Process Description**

Define and communicate quality requirements in all processes, procedures and the related enterprise outcomes, including controls, ongoing monitoring, and the use of proven practices and standards in continuous improvement and efficiency efforts.

**Process Purpose Statement**

Ensure consistent delivery of solutions and services to meet the quality requirements of the enterprise and satisfy stakeholder needs.

**The process supports the achievement of a set of IT-related goals, which support the achievement of a set of enterprise goals:**

| Ref | IT-related Goal |
|---|---|
| 05 | Realized benefits from IT-enabled investments and services portfolio |
| 07 | Delivery of IT services in line with business requirements |
| 13 | Delivery of programs on time, on budget, and meeting requirements and quality standards |

## APO12: Manage Risk

| APO12 | Manage Risk | Domain: | Management |
|---|---|---|---|
| | | Area: | Align, Plan, & Organize |

**Process Description**

Continually identify, assess, and reduce IT-related risk within levels of tolerance set by enterprise executive management.

**Process Purpose Statement**

Integrate the management of IT-related enterprise risk with overall ERM, and balance the costs and benefits of managing IT-related enterprise risk.

**The process supports the achievement of a set of IT-related goals, which support the achievement of a set of enterprise goals:**

| Ref | IT-related Goal |
|---|---|
| 02 | IT compliance and support for business compliance with external laws and regulations |
| 04 | Managed IT-related business risks |
| 06 | Transparency of IT costs, benefits and risk |
| 10 | Security of information and processing infrastructure and applications |
| 13 | Delivery of programs on time, on budget and meeting requirements and quality standards |

## APO13: Manage Security

| APO13 | Manage Security | Domain: | Management |
|---|---|---|---|
| | | Area: | Align, Plan, & Organize |
| **Process Description** | | | |
| Define, operate, and monitor a system for information security management. | | | |
| **Process Purpose Statement** | | | |
| Keep the impact and occurrence of information security incidents within the enterprise's risk appetite levels | | | |
| The process supports the achievement of a set of IT-related goals, which support the achievement of a set of enterprise goals: | | | |
| Ref | IT-related Goal | | |
| 02 | IT compliance and support for business compliance with external laws and regulations | | |
| 04 | Managed IT-related business risks | | |
| 06 | Transparency of IT costs, benefits and risk | | |
| 10 | Security of information and processing infrastructure and applications | | |
| 14 | Availability of reliable and useful information for decision making | | |

# 5.7 Management Domain: Build, Acquire & Implement

- BAI01 Manage programs and projects
- BAI02 Manage requirements definition
- BAI03 Manage solutions identification and build
- BAI04 Manage availability and capacity
- BAI05 Manage organizational change enablement
- BAI06 Manage changes
- BAI07 Manage change acceptance and transitioning
- BAI08 Manage knowledge
- BAI09 Manage assets
- BAI10 Manage configuration

## BAI01: Manage Programs and Projects

| BAI01 | Manage Programs and Projects | Domain: | Management |
| --- | --- | --- | --- |
| | | Area: | Build, Acquire & Implement |
| **Process Description** | | | |
| Manage all programs and projects from the investment portfolio in alignment with enterprise strategy and in a coordinated way. Initiate, plan, control and execute programs and projects and close with a post-implementation review | | | |
| **Process Purpose Statement** | | | |
| Realize business benefits and reduce the risk of unexpected delays, costs and value erosion by improving communications to and involvement of business and end users, ensuring the value and quality of project deliverables and maximizing their contribution to the investment and services portfolio | | | |
| **The process supports the achievement of a set of IT-related goals, which support the achievement of a set of enterprise goals:** | | | |
| Ref | IT-related Goal | | |
| 01 | Alignment of IT and business strategy | | |
| 04 | Managed IT-related business risks | | |
| 05 | Realized benefits from IT-enabled investments and services portfolio | | |
| 13 | Delivery of programs on time, on budget and meeting requirements and quality standards | | |

## BAI02: Manage requirements definition

| BAI02 | Manage requirements definition | Domain: | Management |
| --- | --- | --- | --- |
| | | Area: | Build, Acquire & Implement |
| **Process Description** | | | |
| Identify solutions and analyse requirements before acquisition or creation to ensure that they are in line with enterprise strategic requirements covering business processes, applications, information/ data, infrastructure, and services. Coordinate with affected stakeholders the review of feasible options including relative costs and benefits, risk analysis, and approval of requirements and proposed solutions | | | |
| **Process Purpose Statement** | | | |
| Create feasible optimal solutions that meet enterprise needs while minimizing risks | | | |
| **The process supports the achievement of a set of IT-related goals, which support the achievement of a set of enterprise goals:** | | | |
| Ref | IT-related Goal | | |
| 01 | Alignment of IT and business strategy | | |
| 07 | Delivery of IT services in line with business requirements | | |
| 12 | Enablement and support of business processes by integrating applications and technology into business processes | | |

## BAI03: Manage solutions identification and build

| BAI03 | Manage solutions identification and build | Domain: | Management |
|---|---|---|---|
| | | Area: | Build, Acquire & Implement |

**Process Description**

Establish and maintain identified solutions in line with enterprise requirements covering design, development, and procurement/sourcing, and partnering with suppliers/vendors. Manage configurations, test preparation, testing, requirements management, and maintenance of business processes, applications, information/data, infrastructure, and services.

**Process Purpose Statement**

Establish timely and cost effective solutions capable of supporting enterprise strategic and operational objectives.

The process supports the achievement of a set of IT-related goals, which support the achievement of a set of enterprise goals:

| Ref | IT-related Goal |
|---|---|
| 07 | Delivery of IT services in line with business requirements |

## BAI04: Manage Availability & Capacity

| BAI04 | Manage Availability & Capacity | Domain: | Management |
|---|---|---|---|
| | | Area: | Build, Acquire & Implement |

**Process Description**

Balance current and future needs for availability, performance, and capacity with cost-effective service provision. Include assessment of current capabilities, forecasting of future needs based on business requirements, analysis of business impacts, and assessment of risk to plan and implement actions to meet the identified requirements.

**Process Purpose Statement**

Maintain service availability, efficient management of resources, and optimisation of system performance through prediction of future performance and capacity requirements.

The process supports the achievement of a set of IT-related goals, which support the achievement of a set of enterprise goals:

| Ref | IT-related Goal |
|---|---|
| 07 | Delivery of IT services in line with business requirements |
| 11 | Optimization of IT assets, resources, and capabilities |
| 14 | Availability of reliable and useful information for decision making |

## BAI05: Manage organizational change enablement

| BAI05 | Manage organizational change enablement | Domain: | Management |
|---|---|---|---|
| | | Area: | Build, Acquire & Implement |
| **Process Description** | | | |
| Maximise the likelihood of successfully implementing sustainable enterprise wide organisational change quickly and with reduced risk, covering the complete life cycle of the change and all affected stakeholders in the business and IT. | | | |
| **Process Purpose Statement** | | | |
| Prepare and commit stakeholders for business change and reduce the risk of failure. | | | |
| **The process supports the achievement of a set of IT-related goals, which support the achievement of a set of enterprise goals:** | | | |
| Ref | IT-related Goal | | |
| 08 | Adequate usage of applications, information and technology solutions | | |
| 13 | Delivery of programs on time, on budget and meeting requirements and quality standards | | |
| 17 | Knowledge, expertise and initiatives for business innovation | | |

## BAI06: Manage Changes

| BAI06 | Manage Changes | Domain: | Management |
|---|---|---|---|
| | | Area: | Build, Acquire & Implement |
| **Process Description** | | | |
| Manage all changes in a controlled manner, including standard changes and emergency maintenance relating to business processes, applications, and infrastructure. This includes change standards and procedures, impact assessment, prioritisation and authorisation, emergency changes, tracking, reporting, closure and documentation. | | | |
| **Process Purpose Statement** | | | |
| Enable fast and reliable delivery of change to the business and mitigation of the risk of negatively impacting the stability or integrity of the changed environment. | | | |
| **The process supports the achievement of a set of IT-related goals, which support the achievement of a set of enterprise goals:** | | | |
| Ref | IT-related Goal | | |
| 04 | Managed IT-related business risks | | |
| 07 | Delivery of IT services in line with business requirements | | |
| 10 | Security of information and processing infrastructure and applications | | |

## BAI07: Manage change acceptance and transitioning

| BAI07 | Manage change acceptance and transitioning | Domain: | Management |
|---|---|---|---|
| | | Area: | Build, Acquire & Implement |

**Process Description**

Formally accept and make operational new solutions, including implementation planning, system and data conversion, acceptance testing, communication, release preparation, promotion to production of new or changed business processes and IT services, early production support, and a post-implementation review.

**Process Purpose Statement**

Implement solutions safely and in line with the agreed-on expectations and outcomes.

**The process supports the achievement of a set of IT-related goals, which support the achievement of a set of enterprise goals:**

| Ref | IT-related Goal |
|---|---|
| 08 | Adequate usage of applications, information and technology solutions |
| 12 | Enablement and support of business processes by integrating applications and technology into business processes |

## BAI08: Manage Knowledge

| BAI08 | Manage Knowledge | Domain: | Management |
|---|---|---|---|
| | | Area: | Build, Acquire & Implement |

**Process Description**

Maintain the availability of relevant, current, validated, and reliable knowledge to support all process activities and to facilitate decision making. Plan for the identification, gathering, organising, maintaining, use and retirement of knowledge.

**Process Purpose Statement**

Provide the knowledge required to support all staff in their work activities and for informed decision making and enhanced productivity.

**The process supports the achievement of a set of IT-related goals, which support the achievement of a set of enterprise goals:**

| Ref | IT-related Goal |
|---|---|
| 09 | IT agility |
| 17 | Knowledge, expertise and initiatives for business innovation |

## BAI09: Manage Assets

| BAI09 | Manage Assets | Domain: | Management |
|---|---|---|---|
| | | Area: | Build, Acquire & Implement |

**Process Description**

Manage IT assets through their life cycle to make sure that their use delivers value at optimal cost, they remain operational (fit for purpose), they are accounted for and physically protected, and those assets that are critical to support service capability are reliable and available. Manage software licences to ensure that the optimal number are acquired, retained, and deployed in relation to required business usage, and the software installed is in compliance with licence agreements.

**Process Purpose Statement**

Account for all IT assets and optimise the value provided by these assets.

**The process supports the achievement of a set of IT-related goals, which support the achievement of a set of enterprise goals:**

| Ref | IT-related Goal |
|---|---|
| 06 | Transparency of IT costs, benefits and risk |
| 11 | Optimization of IT assets, resources, and capabilities |

## BAI10: Manage Configuration

| BAI10 | Manage Configuration | Domain: | Management |
|---|---|---|---|
| | | Area: | Build, Acquire & Implement |

**Process Description**

Define and maintain descriptions and relationships between key resources and capabilities required to deliver IT-enabled services, including collecting configuration information, establishing baselines, verifying and auditing configuration information, and updating the configuration repository.

**Process Purpose Statement**

Provide sufficient information about service assets to enable the service to be effectively managed, assess the impact of changes and deal with service Incidents.

**The process supports the achievement of a set of IT-related goals, which support the achievement of a set of enterprise goals:**

| Ref | IT-related Goal |
|---|---|
| 02 | IT compliance and support for business compliance with external laws and regulations |
| 11 | Optimization of IT assets, resources, and capabilities |
| 14 | Availability of reliable and useful information for decision making |

# 5.8 Management Domain: Deliver, Service & Support

- DSS01 Manage operations
- DSS02 Manage service requests and incidents
- DSS03 Manage problems
- DSS04 Manage continuity
- DSS05 Manage security services
- DSS06 Manage business process controls

## DSS01: Manage Operations

| DSS01 | Manage Operations | Domain: | Management |
|-------|-------------------|---------|------------|
| | | Area: | Deliver, Service & Support |
| **Process Description** | | | |
| Co-ordinate and execute the activities and operational procedures required to deliver internal and outsourced IT services, including the execution of pre-defined standard operating procedures and the required monitoring activities. | | | |
| **Process Purpose Statement** | | | |
| Deliver IT operational service outcomes as planned | | | |
| **The process supports the achievement of a set of IT-related goals, which support the achievement of a set of enterprise goals:** | | | |
| **Ref** | **IT-related Goal** | | |
| 04 | Managed IT-related business risks | | |
| 07 | Delivery of IT services in line with business requirements | | |
| 11 | Optimization of IT assets, resources and capabilities | | |

## DSS02: Manage Service Requests and Incidents

| DSS02 | Manage Service Requests and Incidents | Domain: | Management |
|-------|---------------------------------------|---------|------------|
| | | Area: | Deliver, Service & Support |
| **Process Description** | | | |
| Provide timely and effective response to user requests and resolution of all types of incidents. Restore normal service; record and fulfil user requests; and record, investigate, diagnose, escalate and resolve incidents. | | | |
| **Process Purpose Statement** | | | |
| Achieve increased productivity and minimise disruptions through quick resolution of user queries and incidents. | | | |
| **The process supports the achievement of a set of IT-related goals, which support the achievement of a set of enterprise goals:** | | | |
| **Ref** | **IT-related Goal** | | |
| 04 | Managed IT-related business risks | | |
| 07 | Delivery of IT services in line with business requirements | | |

## DSS03: Manage Problems

| DSS03 | Manage Problems | Domain: | Management |
|---|---|---|---|
| | | Area: | Deliver, Service & Support |

**Process Description**

Identify and classify problems and their root causes and provide timely resolution to prevent recurring incidents. Provide recommendations for improvements.

**Process Purpose Statement**

Increase availability, improve service levels, reduce costs, and improve customer convenience and satisfaction by reducing the number of operational problems.

**The process supports the achievement of a set of IT-related goals, which support the achievement of a set of enterprise goals:**

| Ref | IT-related Goal |
|---|---|
| 04 | Managed IT-related business risks |
| 07 | Delivery of IT services in line with business requirements |
| 11 | Optimization of IT assets, resources and capabilities |
| 14 | Availability of reliable and useful information for decision making |

## DSS04: Manage Continuity

| DSS04 | Manage Continuity | Domain: | Management |
|---|---|---|---|
| | | Area: | Deliver, Service & Support |

**Process Description**

Establish and maintain a plan to enable the business and IT to respond to incidents and disruptions in order to continue operation of critical business processes and required IT services and maintain availability of information at a level acceptable to the enterprise.

**Process Purpose Statement**

Continue critical business operations and maintain availability of information at a level acceptable to the enterprise in the event of a significant disruption.

**The process supports the achievement of a set of IT-related goals, which support the achievement of a set of enterprise goals:**

| Ref | IT-related Goal |
|---|---|
| 04 | Managed IT-related business risks |
| 07 | Delivery of IT services in line with business requirements |
| 14 | Availability of reliable and useful information for decision making |

## DSS05: Manage Security Services

| DSS05 | Manage Security Services | Domain: | Management |
|---|---|---|---|
| | | Area: | Deliver, Service & Support |

**Process Description**

Protect enterprise information to maintain the level of information security risk acceptable to the enterprise in accordance with the security policy. Establish and maintain information security roles and access privileges and perform security monitoring.

**Process Purpose Statement**

Minimise the business impact of operational information security vulnerabilities and incidents.

**The process supports the achievement of a set of IT-related goals, which support the achievement of a set of enterprise goals:**

| Ref | IT-related Goal |
|---|---|
| 02 | IT compliance and support for business compliance with external laws and regulations |
| 04 | Managed IT-related business risks |
| 10 | Security of information and processing infrastructure and applications |

## DSS06: Manage Business Process Controls

| DSS06 | Manage Business Process Controls | Domain: | Management |
|---|---|---|---|
| | | Area: | Deliver, Service & Support |

**Process Description**

Define and maintain appropriate business process controls to ensure that information related to and processed by in-house or outsourced business processes satisfies all relevant information control requirements. Identify the relevant information control requirements and manage and operate adequate controls to ensure that information and information processing satisfy these requirements.

**Process Purpose Statement**

Maintain information integrity and the security of information assets handled within business processes in the enterprise or outsourced

**The process supports the achievement of a set of IT-related goals, which support the achievement of a set of enterprise goals:**

| Ref | IT-related Goal |
|---|---|
| 04 | Managed IT-related business risks |
| 07 | Delivery of IT services in line with business requirements |

## 5.9   Management Domain: Monitor, Evaluate & Assure

- MEA01 Monitor, evaluate and assess performance and conformance
- MEA02 Monitor, evaluate and assess the system of internal control
- MEA03 Monitor, evaluate and assess compliance with external requirements

### MEA01: Monitor, evaluate and assess performance and conformance

| MEA01 | Monitor, evaluate and assess performance and conformance | Domain: | Management |
|---|---|---|---|
| | | Area: | Monitor, Evaluate & Assure |
| **Process Description** | | | |
| Collect, validate and evaluate business, IT and process goals and metrics. Monitor that processes are performing against agreed-on performance and conformance goals and metrics and provide reporting that is systematic and timely. | | | |
| **Process Purpose Statement** | | | |
| Provide transparency of performance and compliance and drive achievement of goals | | | |
| **The process supports the achievement of a set of IT-related goals, which support the achievement of a set of enterprise goals:** | | | |
| **Ref** | **IT-related Goal** | | |
| 04 | Managed IT-related business risks | | |
| 07 | Delivery of IT services in line with business requirements | | |
| 11 | Optimization of IT assets, resources, and capabilities | | |
| 15 | IT compliance with internal policies | | |

### MEA02: Monitor, evaluate and assess the system of internal control

| MEA02 | Monitor, evaluate and assess the system of internal control | Domain: | Management |
|---|---|---|---|
| | | Area: | Monitor, Evaluate & Assure |
| **Process Description** | | | |
| Continuously monitor and evaluate the control environment, including self-assessments and independent assurance reviews. Enable management to identify control deficiencies and inefficiencies and to initiate improvement actions. Plan, organise, and maintain standards for internal control assessment and assurance activities. | | | |
| **Process Purpose Statement** | | | |
| Obtain transparency for key stakeholders on the adequacy of the system of internal controls and thus provide trust in operations, confidence in the achievement of enterprise objectives and an adequate understanding of residual risks. | | | |
| **The process supports the achievement of a set of IT-related goals, which support the achievement of a set of enterprise goals:** | | | |
| **Ref** | **IT-related Goal** | | |
| 02 | IT compliance and support for business compliance with external laws and regulations | | |
| 04 | Managed IT-related business risks | | |
| 15 | IT compliance with internal policies | | |

## MEA03: Monitor, evaluate and assess compliance with external requirements

| MEA03 | Monitor, evaluate and assess compliance with external requirements | Domain: | Management |
|---|---|---|---|
| | | Area: | Monitor, Evaluate & Assure |
| **Process Description** | | | |
| Evaluate that IT processes and IT-supported business processes are compliant with laws, regulations, and contractual requirements. Obtain assurance that the requirements have been identified and complied with, and integrate IT compliance with overall enterprise compliance. | | | |
| **Process Purpose Statement** | | | |
| Ensure that the enterprise is compliant with all applicable external requirements. | | | |
| **The process supports the achievement of a set of IT-related goals, which support the achievement of a set of enterprise goals:** | | | |
| **Ref** | **IT-related Goal** | | |
| 02 | External compliance requirements are adequately addressed | | |
| 04 | Managed IT-related business risks | | |

# CHAPTER 6

# Implementation guidance

## 6.1 Introduction

Optimal value can only be realized from leveraging COBIT if it is effectively adopted and adapted to suit each enterprise's unique environment. Each implementation approach will also need to address specific challenges including managing changes to culture and behavior. ISACA provides practical and extensive implementation guidance in its publication COBIT 5: *Implementation Guide*[29] which is based on a continual improvement lifecycle. It is not intended to be a prescriptive approach nor a complete solution, but rather a guide to avoid commonly encountered pitfalls, leverage best practices and assist in the creation of successful outcomes. The guide is also supported by an implementation toolkit containing a variety of resources that will be continually enhanced. Its content includes:
- Self-assessment, measurement, and diagnostic tools
- Presentations aimed at various audiences
- Related articles and further explanations

The purpose of this section is to introduce the implementation and continual improvement lifecycle at a high level and to highlight a number of important topics from COBIT 5: *Implementation Guide,* such as:
- Making a business case for the implementation and improvement of the governance and management of IT
- Recognizing typical pain-points and event triggers

---

29 www.isaca.org/cobit/Documents/COBIT-5-Implementation-Introduction.pdf

- The creation of the right environment for implementation
- Leveraging COBIT to identify gaps and guide the development of enablers such as policies, processes, principles, organizational structures and roles and responsibilities

## 6.2  Considering the IT organization context

The governance and management of enterprise IT do not occur in a vacuum. Every enterprise needs to design its own implementation plan or road map, depending on factors in the enterprise's specific internal and external environment, such as:

- Ethics and culture
- Applicable laws, regulations, and policies
- Mission, vision and values
- Governance policies and practices
- Business plan and strategic intentions
- Operating model and level of maturity
- Management style
- Risk appetite
- Capabilities and available resources
- Industry practices

It is equally important to leverage and build on any governance and management of IT enablers that the enterprise already has in place. The optimal approach for the governance and management of enterprise IT will be different for every enterprise; the context needs to be understood and considered in order to adopt and adapt COBIT effectively in the implementation of governance and management of enterprise IT enablers. COBIT is often underpinned with other frameworks, best practices and standards and these too need to be adapted to suit specific requirements.

Key success factors for successful implementation include:

- Top management providing the direction and mandate for the initiative, as well as visible ongoing commitment and support
- All parties supporting the governance and management processes to understand the business and IT objectives
- Ensuring effective communication and enablement of the necessary changes

- Tailoring COBIT and other supporting best practices and standards to fit the unique context of the enterprise
- Focusing on quick wins and prioritizing the most beneficial improvements that are easiest to implement

## 6.3 Creating the right environment

It is important for implementation initiatives leveraging COBIT to be properly governed and adequately managed. Major IT-related initiatives often fail due to inadequate direction, support, and oversight by the various required stakeholders; the implementation of governance or management of IT enablers leveraging COBIT is no different. Support and direction from key stakeholders are critical so that improvements are adopted and sustained. In a weak enterprise environment (such as an unclear overall business operating model or lack of enterprise-level governance enablers), this support, and participation are even more important.

Enablers leveraging COBIT should be a solution addressing real business needs and issues rather than an end in themselves. Requirements based on current pain points and drivers should be identified and accepted by management as areas that need to be addressed. High-level health checks, diagnostics, or capability assessments based on COBIT are excellent tools to raise awareness, create consensus and generate a commitment to act. The commitment and buy-in of the relevant stakeholders need to be solicited from the beginning. To achieve this, implementation objectives and benefits need to be clearly expressed in business terms and summarized in an outline business case.

Once commitment has been obtained, adequate resources need to be provided to support the program. Key program roles and responsibilities should be defined and assigned. Care should be taken on an ongoing basis to maintain commitment from all affected stakeholders. Appropriate structures and processes for oversight and direction should be established and maintained. These structures and processes should also ensure ongoing alignment with enterprise-wide governance and risk management approaches. Last, visible support and commitment should be provided by key stakeholders such as the board and executives to set the "tone at the top" and ensure commitment for the program at all levels.

## 6.4   Recognizing pain-points and event triggers

There are a number of factors that may indicate a need for improved governance and management of enterprise IT. By using pain-points or event triggers as the launching point for implementation initiatives, the business case for governance or management of enterprise IT improvement can be related to practical, everyday issues being experienced. Examples of some of the typical pain-points for which new or revised governance or management of IT enablers can be a solution (or part of a solution) are:

• Business frustration with failed initiatives, rising IT costs and a perception of low business value
• Significant incidents related to IT risk, such as data loss or project failure
• Outsourcing service delivery problems, such as consistent failure to meet agreed service levels
• Failure to meet regulatory or contractual requirements
• IT limiting the enterprise's innovation capabilities and business agility
• Regular audit findings about poor IT performance or reported IT quality of service problems
• Hidden and rogue IT spending
• Duplication or overlap between initiatives or wasting resources, such as premature project termination
• Insufficient IT resources, staff with inadequate skills or staff burn-out/ dissatisfaction
• IT-enabled changes failing to meet business needs and delivered late or over budget
• Board members, executives, or senior managers who are reluctant to engage with IT, or a lack of committed and satisfied business sponsors for IT
• Complex IT operating models

In addition to these pain-points, other events in the enterprise's internal and external environment can signal or trigger a focus on the governance and management of IT. Examples of these from the guide are:

• Merger, acquisition or divestiture
• A shift in the market, economy, or competitive position
• Change in business operating model or sourcing arrangements
• New regulatory or compliance requirements
• Significant technology change or paradigm shift
• An enterprise-wide governance focus or project
• A new CxO

- External audit or consultant assessments
- A new business strategy or priority

## 6.5 Enabling change

Successful implementation depends on implementing the right change (the right governance or management enablers) in the right way. In many enterprises, there is a significant focus on the first aspect – core governance or management of IT – but not enough emphasis on managing the human, behavioral, and cultural aspects of the change and motivating stakeholders to buy into the change. It should not be assumed that the various stakeholders involved in, or affected by, new or revised enablers will readily accept and adopt the change. The possibility of ignorance and/or resistance to change needs to be addressed through a structured and proactive approach. Also, optimal awareness of the implementation program should be achieved through a communication plan that defines what will be communicated, in what way and by whom, throughout the various phases of the program. Sustainable improvement can be achieved either by gaining the commitment of the stakeholders (investment in winning hearts and minds, in leaders' time, and in communicating and responding to the workforce) or, where still required, by enforcing compliance (investment in processes to administer, monitor and enforce). In other words, human, behavioral, and cultural barriers need to be overcome so that there is a common interest to properly adopt a new way, instill a will to adopt a new way, and to ensure the ability to adopt a new way.

## 6.6 A lifecycle approach

The implementation lifecycle provides a way for enterprises to address the complexity and challenges typically encountered during implementations using COBIT. There are three inter-related components to the lifecycle:
1. The core continual improvement lifecycle – this is not a one-off project
2. The enablement of change (addressing the behavioral and cultural aspects)
3. The management of the program

The right environment needs to be created to ensure the success of the implementation or improvement initiative. The lifecycle and its seven phases are illustrated in Figure 6.1.

**Phase 1** starts with recognizing and agreeing to the need for an implementation or improvement initiative. It identifies the current pain-points and triggers and creates a desire to change at executive management levels.

**Phase 2** is focused on defining the scope of the implementation or improvement initiative using COBIT's mapping of enterprise goals to IT-related goals to the associated IT processes. High-level diagnostics can also be useful for scoping and understanding high-priority areas on which to focus. An assessment of the current state is then performed, and issues or deficiencies are identified. Large-scale initiatives should be structured as multiple iterations of the lifecycle – for any implementation initiative exceeding six months there is a risk of losing momentum, focus, and buy-in from stakeholders.

During **Phase 3**, an improvement target is set, followed by a more detailed analysis leveraging COBIT's guidance to identify gaps and potential solutions. Some solutions may be quick wins and others more challenging and longer-term activities. Priority should be given to initiatives that are easier to achieve and those likely to yield the greatest benefits.

**Phase 4** plans practical solutions by defining projects supported by justifiable business cases. A change plan for implementation is also developed. A well-developed business case helps to ensure that the project's benefits are identified and monitored.

The proposed solutions are implemented into day-to-day practices **in Phase 5**. Measures can be defined and monitoring established, using COBIT's goals and metrics to ensure that business alignment is achieved and maintained and performance can be measured. Success requires the engagement and demonstrated commitment of top management as well as ownership by the affected business and IT stakeholders.

**Phase 6** focuses on the sustainable operation of the new or improved enablers and the monitoring of the achievement of expected benefits.

**During phase 7**, the overall success of the initiative is reviewed, further requirements for the governance or management of enterprise IT are identified, and the need for continual improvement is reinforced. Over time, the lifecycle should be followed iteratively while building a sustainable approach to the governance and management of enterprise IT.

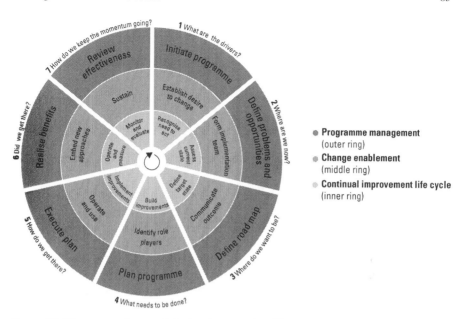

**Figure 6.1** The seven phases of the implementation lifecycle

Source Figure 17, The Seven Phases of the Information Lifecyle, COBIT 5: A Business Framework for the Governance and Management of Enterprise IT, 2012 © ISACA.

## 6.7  Getting started: making the business case

To ensure the success of implementation initiatives leveraging COBIT, the need to act should be widely recognized and communicated within the enterprise. This can be in the form of a "wake-up call" (where specific pain-points are being experienced, as discussed previously) or an expression of the improvement opportunity to be pursued and, very important, the benefits that will be realized. An appropriate level of urgency needs to be instilled and the key stakeholders should be aware of the risks of not taking action as well as the benefits of undertaking the program. The initiative should be owned by a sponsor, involve all key stakeholders and be based on a business case. Initially this can be at a high level from a strategic perspective – from the top down – starting with a clear understanding of the desired business outcomes and progressing to a detailed description of critical tasks and milestones as well as key roles and responsibilities. The business case is a valuable tool available to management in guiding the creation of business value. At a minimum, the business case should include the following:

- The business benefits targeted their alignment with business strategy and the associated benefit owners (who in the business will be responsible for securing them). This could be based on pain-points and event triggers.

- The business changes needed to create the envisioned value. This could be based on health-checks and capability gap analyzes and should clearly state both what is in scope and what is out of scope.
- The investments needed to make the governance and management of enterprise IT changes (based on estimates of projects required)
- The ongoing IT and business costs
- The expected benefits of operating in the changed way
- The risks inherent in the previous bullet points, including any constraints or dependencies (based on challenges and success factors)
- Roles, responsibilities and accountabilities related to the initiative
- How the investment and value creation will be monitored throughout the economic lifecycle, and the metrics to be used (based on goals and metrics)

The business case is not a one-time static document. It is a dynamic operational tool that must be continually updated to reflect the current view of the future, so that a view of the viability of the program can be maintained.

It can be difficult to quantify the benefits of implementation or improvement initiatives, and care should be taken to commit only to benefits that are realistic and achievable. Studies conducted across a number of enterprises could provide useful information on benefits that have been achieved.

A study conducted across 250 enterprises worldwide found that those enterprises with superior governance of enterprise IT had at least 20 percent higher profitability than enterprises with poor governance given the same objectives.[30] It argues that IT business value results directly from effective governance of enterprise IT. Finally, another case research in the airline industry concluded that the implementation and ongoing assurance of organizational governance of IT restored trust between business and IT, and resulted in an increased alignment of investments to strategic goals. Also, more tangible benefits were reported in this case, including lowered IT continuity cost per business production unit, and the freeing up of funds for innovation. Other cross-case research in the financial sector demonstrated that enterprises with better governance of IT approaches clearly obtained higher maturity scores in business/IT alignment.[31]

---

30 Weill, P.; Jeanne W. Ross; Governance of enterprise IT: How Top Performers Manage IT Decision Rights for Superior Results, Harvard Business School Press, USA, 2004
31 De Haes, Steven; Dirk Gemke; John Thorp; Wim Van Grembergen; "Analysing IT Value Management @ KLM Through the Lens of Val IT", ISCACA Journal, vol. 4, USA, 2011. Van Grembergen, Wim; Steven De Haes; Enterprise Governance of IT: Achieving Alignment and Value; Springer, USA, 2009

# CHAPTER 7

# The process capability model

## 7.1 Introduction

The COBIT 4.1, Risk IT, and Val IT models are used to measure the current or "as-is" maturity of an enterprise's IT-related processes, to define a required "to-be" state of maturity, to determine the gap between them and how to improve the process to achieve the desired maturity level. The COBIT 5 product set includes a new process capability model, based on the internationally recognized ISO/IEC 15504 Software Engineering – Process Assessment standard. This model will achieve the same overall objectives of process assessment and process improvement support. However, the new model is different from the COBIT 4.1 maturity model in its design and use.

In this section, the following topics are discussed:
- Differences between the new COBIT 5 and the COBIT 4 models
- Benefits of the COBIT 5 model
- Summary of the differences COBIT 5 users will encounter in practice
- Performing a COBIT 5 capability assessment

Although this approach will provide valuable information about the state of processes, processes are one of the seven governance and management enablers. In consequence, process assessments will not provide the full picture on the state of governance of an enterprise. For that, the other enablers need to be assessed as well.

The elements of the COBIT 4 maturity model approach are shown in Figure 7.1.

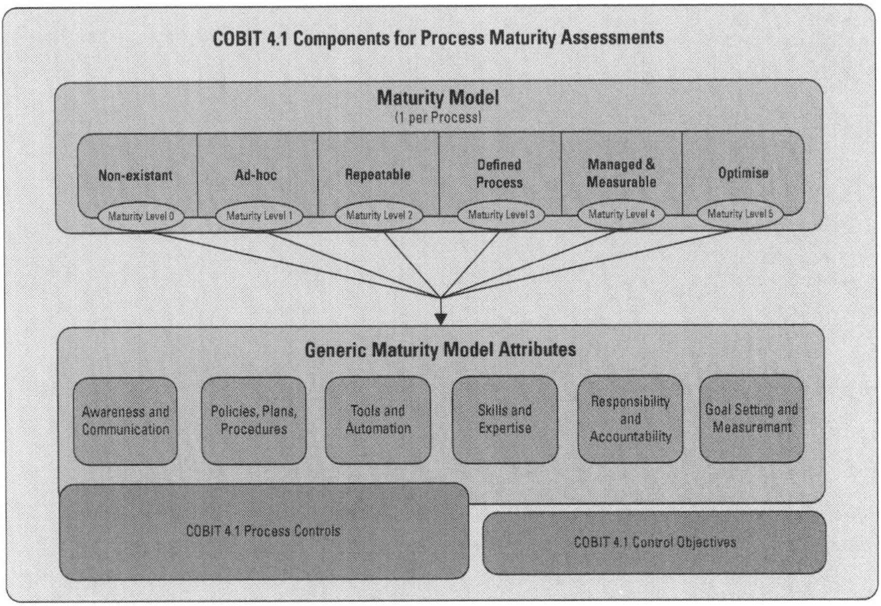

Figure 7.1 Summary of the COBIT 4.1 process maturity model

Using the COBIT 4.1 maturity model for process improvement purposes – assessing a process maturity, defining a target maturity level, and identifying the gaps – required using the following COBIT 4.1 components:

- First, an assessment needed to be made whether control objectives for the process were met.
- Next, the maturity model included in the management guideline for each process could be used to obtain a maturity profile of the process.
- In addition, the generic maturity model in COBIT 4.1 provided six distinct attributes that were applicable for each process and that assisted in obtaining a more detailed view on the processes" maturity level.
- Process controls are generic control objectives – they also needed to be reviewed when a process assessment was made. Process controls partially overlap with the generic maturity model attributes.

The process capability approach is presented in Figure 7.2.

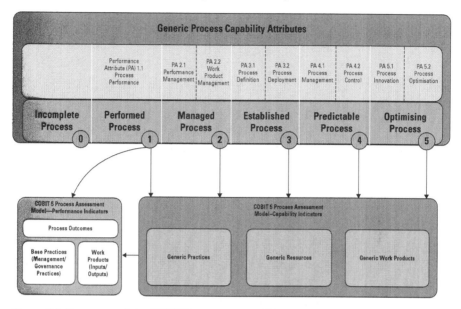

Figure 7.2  Summary of the COBIT 5 process capability model
Source Figure 19, Summary of the COBIT 5 Process Capability Model, COBIT 5: A Business Framework for the Governance and Management of Enterprise IT, 2012 © ISACA.

The main process capability model characteristics follow:
There are six levels of capability a process can achieve, including an "incomplete process" designation if the practices in it do not achieve the intended purpose of the process:
0. Incomplete process
1. Performed process (one attribute)
2. Managed process (two attributes)
3. Established process (two attributes)
4. Predictable process (two attributes)
5. Optimizing process (two attributes)

The most important differences between an ISO/IEC 15504-based process capability assessment and the COBIT 4.1 maturity model (or, for that matter, of the Val IT and Risk IT domain-based maturity models) can be summarized as follows:

- The naming and meaning of the ISO/IEC 15504-defined capability levels are quite different from the current COBIT 4.1 maturity levels for processes.
- In ISO/IEC 15504, capability levels are defined by a set of nine process attributes
- Requirements for an ISO/IEC15504:2-compliant process reference model prescribe that in the description of any process that will be assessed:
  o The process is described in terms of its purpose and outcomes.
  o The process description shall not contain any aspects of the measurement framework beyond level 1, which means that any characteristic of a process attribute beyond level 1 cannot appear inside a process description

## 7.2  Benefits of the changes

The benefits of the new COBIT 5 process capability model, compared to the COBIT 4.1 maturity models, include:

- Improved focus on the process being performed
- Simplification through elimination of duplication of content
- Improved reliability and repeatability of process capability assessment activities and evaluations
- Compliance with a generally accepted process assessment standard
- Increased usability of process capability assessment results

## 7.3  Performing process capability assessments

The ISO/IEC 15504 standard specifies that process capability assessments can be performed for various purposes and with varying degrees of rigor. Purposes can be internal, with a focus on comparisons between enterprise areas and/or process improvement for internal benefit, or they can be external, with a focus on formal assessment, reporting, and certification.

The COBIT 5 ISO 15504-based assessment approach continues to facilitate the following objectives that have been a key COBIT management tools approach since 2000 to

- Enable management to benchmark process capability.
- Enable high-level "as-is" and "to-be" health-checks to support management investment decision-making with regard to process improvement.
- Provide gap analysis and improvement planning information to support definition of justifiable improvement projects.
- Provide management with assessment ratings so they can measure and monitor current capabilities.

This section describes how a high-level assessment can be performed with the new COBIT 5 process capability model to achieve these objectives. The assessment distinguishes between assessing capability level 1 and the higher levels. Process capability level 1 describes whether a process achieves its intended purpose, and is therefore a very important level to achieve – as well as foundational in enabling higher capability levels to be reached. Assessing whether the process achieves its goals – or, in other words, achieves capability level 1 – can be done by:

1. Reviewing the process outcomes as they are described for each process in the detailed process descriptions, and using the ISO/IEC 15504 rating scale to assign a rating to which degree each objective is achieved. This scale consists of the following ratings:

| N | Not achieved | 0 to 15% achievement |
|---|---|---|
| P | Partially achieved | 15 to 50% achievement |
| L | Largely achieved | 50 to 85% achievement |
| F | Fully achieved | 85 to 100% achievement |

2. In addition, the process (governance or management) practices can be assessed using the same rating scale, expressing to which extent the base practices are applied.
3. To further refine the assessment, the work products may be taken into consideration as well to determine to which extent a specific assessment attribute has been achieved.

Although defining target capability levels is up to each enterprise to decide, many enterprises will have the ambition to have all their processes achieve capability level 1 (otherwise, what would be the point of having these processes?). If this level is not achieved, the reasons for not achieving this level are immediately obvious from the approach explained above, and an improvement plan can be defined:

1. If a required process outcome is not consistently achieved, the process does not meet its objective and needs to be improved.

2. The assessment of the process practices will reveal which practices are lacking or failing, enabling implementation, and/or improvement of those practices to take place and allowing all process outcomes to be achieved. For higher process capability levels, the generic practices are used, taken from ISO/IEC 15504:2. They provide generic descriptions for each of the capability levels.

# Detailed mappings[32]

## Enterprise goals – IT-related goals

Table B1 contains:

- In the columns, all 17 generic enterprise goals defined in COBIT 5, grouped by BSC dimension
- In the rows, all 17 IT-related goals, also grouped in IT BSC dimensions
- A mapping on how each enterprise goal is supported by IT-related goals. This mapping is expressed using the following scale:
  - "P" stands for primary, when there is an important relationship, i.e., the IT-related goal is a primary support for the enterprise goal.
  - "S" stands for secondary, when there is still a strong, but less important, relationship, i.e., the IT-related goal is a secondary support for the enterprise goal.

---

32 The tables were created based on the following inputs:
   Research by the University of Antwerp Management School (UAMS) IT Alignment and Governance Research Institute
   Additional reviews and expert opinions obtained during the development and review process of COBIT 5

## IT-related goals – IT-related processes

Table B2 contains:

- In the columns, all 17 generic IT-related goals defined in section 3, grouped in IT BSC dimensions
- In the rows, all 36 COBIT 5 processes, grouped by domain
- A mapping on how each IT-related goal is supported by a COBIT 5 IT-related process. This mapping is expressed using the following scale:
  - o "P" stands for primary, when there is an important relationship, i.e., the COBIT 5 process is a primary support for the achievement of an IT-related goal.
  - o "S" stands for secondary, when there is still a strong, but less important, relationship, i.e., the process is a secondary support for the IT-related goal.

**Table B1 Mapping COBIT 5 enterprise goals to IT-related goals**

IT-related goals (columns):

| No. | IT Related Goals | BSC |
|---|---|---|
| 1 | Alignment of IT and business Strategy | Financial |
| 2 | IT compliance and support for business compliance with external laws and regulations | Financial |
| 3 | Commitment of executive management for making IT-related decisions | Financial |
| 4 | Managed IT-related business risks | Financial |
| 5 | Realised benefits from IT-enabled investments and services portfolio | Financial |
| 6 | Transparency of IT costs, benefits and risk | Financial |
| 7 | Delivery of IT services in line with business requirements | Customer |
| 8 | Adequate use of applications, information, and technology solutions | Customer |

Enterprise Goals mapping (P = primary, S = secondary):

| No. | Enterprise Goal | BSC | 1 | 2 | 3 | 4 | 5 | 6 | 7 | 8 |
|---|---|---|---|---|---|---|---|---|---|---|
| 17 | Product and business innovation culture | Learning & Growth | S | | S | | S | | S | S |
| 16 | Skilled and motivated people | Learning & Growth | S | P | S | | S | | S | S |
| 15 | Compliance with internal policies | Internal | | | | | | S | | |
| 14 | Operational and staff productivity | Internal | | | | | | S | | P |
| 13 | Managed business change programmes | Internal | P | | P | | S | | S | |
| 12 | Optimisation of business process costs | Internal | S | | | | P | P | S | S |
| 11 | Optimisation of business process functionality | Internal | P | | P | | S | P | P | P |
| 10 | Optimisation of service delivery costs | Customer | S | | S | | P | S | S | S |
| 9 | Information-based strategic decision making | Customer | P | | P | | | | S | S |
| 8 | Agile responses to changing business environment | Customer | P | | S | | S | S | P | |
| 7 | Business service continuity and availability | Customer | S | | S | | P | | S | S |
| 6 | Customer-oriented service culture | Customer | P | | | | S | | P | S |
| 5 | Financial transparency | Financial | | | | | | P | | |
| 4 | Stakeholder value of business investments | Financial | P | | P | | P | S | P | S |
| 3 | Portfolio of competitive products and services | Financial | P | | S | | P | | P | S |
| 2 | Managed business risks (safeguarding of assets) | Financial | S | S | S | P | | S | S | S |
| 1 | Compliance with external laws and regulations | Financial | | P | S | | | | S | |

| Enterprise Goals | 9 IT agility | 10 Security of information and processing infrastructure and applications | 11 Optimisation of IT assets, resources, and capabilities | 12 Enablement and support of business processes by integrating applications and technology into business processes | 13 Delivery of programmes on time, on budget, and meeting requirements and quality standards | 14 Availability of reliable and useful information | 15 IT compliance with internal policies | 16 Competent and motivated IT personnel | 17 Knowledge, expertise and initiatives for business innovation |
|---|---|---|---|---|---|---|---|---|---|
| Product and business innovation culture | P | | S | S | | | | S | P |
| Skilled and motivated people | S | P | | | | | P | P | S |
| Compliance with internal policies | | | | | | | | | |
| Operational and staff productivity | S | | S | S | S | | | P | S |
| Managed business change programmes | S | | S | S | P | | | | |
| Optimisation of business process costs | | P | S | | S | | | | S |
| Optimisation of business process functionality | P | | S | P | | | S | | |
| Optimisation of service delivery costs | | P | S | | S | | | | S |
| Information-based strategic decision making | | | | | | P | | | |
| Agile responses to changing business environment | P | | S | S | | | | S | P |
| Business service continuity and availability | | P | | | | P | | | |
| Customer-oriented service culture | S | | S | S | | | | S | S |
| Financial transparency | | | | | | | | | |
| Stakeholder value of business investments | S | | P | S | P | S | | S | S |
| Portfolio of competitive products and services | P | | S | P | S | S | | S | P |
| Managed business risks (safeguarding of assets) | S | P | | S | S | S | S | P | |
| Compliance with external laws and regulations | | P | | | | S | S | | |

Internal: columns 9–14. Learning & Growth: columns 15–17.

**Table B2  Mapping COBIT 5 IT-related goals to COBIT 5 processes**

**Enterprise Goals**

| No. | BSC Dimension | Enterprise Goal |
|---|---|---|
| 1 | Corporate | Alignment of IT and business strategy |
| 2 | Corporate | IT compliance and support for business compliance with external laws and regulations |
| 3 | Corporate | Commitment of executive management for making IT-related decisions |
| 4 | Corporate | Managed IT-related business risks |
| 5 | Corporate | Realised benefits from IT-enabled investments and services portfolio |
| 6 | Customer | Transparency of IT costs, benefits and risk |
| 7 | Customer | Delivery of IT services in line with business requirements |
| 8 | Customer | Adequate use of applications, information, and technology solutions |
| 9 | Customer | IT agility |
| 10 | Customer | Security of information and processing infrastructure and applications |
| 11 | Customer | Optimisation of IT assets, resources, and capabilities |
| 12 | Internal | Enablement and support of business processes by integrating applications and technology into business processes |
| 13 | Internal | Delivery of programmes on time, on budget, and meeting requirements and quality standards |
| 14 | Internal | Availability of reliable and useful information |
| 15 | Internal | IT compliance with internal policies |
| 16 | Learning & Growth | Competent and motivated IT personnel |
| 17 | Learning & Growth | Knowledge, expertise and initiatives for business innovation |

**Evaluate, Direct & Monitor / Align, Plan & Organise**

| IT Related Goals | 1 | 2 | 3 | 4 | 5 | 6 | 7 | 8 | 9 | 10 | 11 | 12 | 13 | 14 | 15 | 16 | 17 |
|---|---|---|---|---|---|---|---|---|---|---|---|---|---|---|---|---|---|
| EDM1  Set and Maintain the Governance Framework | P | S | P | S | S | S | P |  | S | S | S | S | S |  | S | S | S |
| EDM2  Ensure Value Optimisation | P |  | S |  | P | P | P | S |  |  | S | S | S |  | S | P |  |
| EDM3  Ensure Risk Optimisation | S | S | S | P | S | P | S | S | P | P | P |  | S | S | P | S | S |
| EDM4  Ensure Resource Optimisation | S |  | S | S | S | S | S | S | S |  | P | S | P | S | S | S |  |
| EDM5  Ensure Stakeholder Transparency | S | P | S | S | S | P | P |  |  |  |  |  | P | S | S |  | S |
| AP01  Define the Management Framework for IT | P | S | S | S | S | S | S | S | P | S | P | S | S | S | P | P | P |
| AP02  Define Strategy | P |  | S |  | S | S | P | S | S |  | S | S |  |  | S | S | P |
| AP03  Manage Enterprise Architecture | P |  | S |  | S |  | S | P | P | S | P | S | S | S | S |  | S |
| AP04  Manage Innovation | P |  | S |  | P |  | S | P | P |  | P | S |  |  |  | P | P |
| AP05  Manage Portfolio | S |  | S | S | P | P | S | S | S |  | P |  | S |  |  |  | S |
| AP06  Manage Budget & Cost |  |  | S |  | P | P | S |  |  |  | P |  | S |  | S |  |  |
| AP07  Manage Human Resources | P |  | S | S | P |  | P | S | P | S | P | S | S |  | S | P | P |
| AP08  Manage Relationships | P |  | S |  | P |  | P | S | P |  | S | S | S |  | S | S | S |
| AP09  Manage Service Agreements | S | S |  |  | S | S | P | S | S | S | S |  |  | S | S |  |  |
| AP010  Manage Suppliers | S | S |  | S | S | S | S | S | S | S | S |  | S | S | S |  | S |
| AP011  Manage Quality | S |  | S | S | S | S | S | S | S | S | S |  | P | S | S | S | S |
| AP012  Manage Risk | S | P | S | P | S | P | S | S | S | P |  |  | P | S | S | S | S |

Legend: P = Primary, S = Secondary

| Enterprise Goals | BAI1 Manage Programmes and Projects | BAI2 Define Requirements | BAI3 Identify & Build Solutions | BAI4 Manage Availability and Capacity | BAI5 Enable Organisational Change | BAI6 Manage Changes | BAI7 Accept & Transition of Change | BAI8 Knowledge Management | DSS1 Manage Operations | DSS2 Manage Assets | DSS3 Manage Configuration | DSS4 Manage Service Requests and Incidents | DSS5 Manage Problems | DSS6 Manage Continuity | DSS7 Manage Security | DSS8 Manage Business Process Cotrols | MEA1 Monitor and Evaluate Performance and Conformance | MEA2 Monitor System of Internal Control | MEA3 Monitor and Evaluate Compliance with External Requirements |
|---|---|---|---|---|---|---|---|---|---|---|---|---|---|---|---|---|---|---|---|
| Knowledge, expertise and initiatives for business innovation | S | S | S |  | S | S |  | P | S |  |  |  | S | S |  | S | S | S | S |
| Competent and motivated IT personnel | S |  |  | S | S |  | S | S | S |  |  | S |  | S | S |  | S | S |  |
| IT compliance with internal policies |  |  |  |  |  | S |  |  | S | S |  |  |  | S | S |  | S | P | P | S |
| Availability of reliable and useful information |  | S | S | S |  | S | S | S | S | S | S | P | P |  |  | S | S | S |  |
| Delivery of programmes on time, on budget, and meeting requirements and quality standards | P | S | S | S | S | S | S |  |  |  |  | S | P |  | S |  |  | S |  |
| Enablement and support of business processes by integrating applications and technology into business processes | P | S |  |  | S | S | S |  |  |  |  |  | P |  | S | S |  |  |  |
| Optimisation of IT assets, resources, and capabilities | S | S | S | P | S | S | P | S | P | P | S |  | P | S |  | P |  |  |  |
| Security of information and processing infrastructure and applications |  | S |  |  |  | S |  | S | S | S | S | S |  | S |  | S | S | S | S |
| IT agility |  | S |  | S | S | S | S | P | S | S | S | S | S |  |  | S |  |  |  |
| Adequate use of applications, information, and technology solutions | S | S | S | S | S | S | S | S | S |  |  | S |  | S | S | P | S | S |  |
| Delivery of IT services in line with business requirements | S | P | P | S | S | S | S | S | S |  | S | S | P |  | P | P | S | P |  |
| Transparency of IT costs, benefits and risk | S |  |  |  | S |  |  |  | P |  |  |  |  | S |  | S | S |  |  |
| Realised benefits from IT-enabled investments and services portfolio | P | S | S | S |  | S | S | S |  |  |  | S | S | S |  | S |  | S |  |
| Managed IT-related business risks | P | S | S | S | P | S |  | P | S | S | P | P | P | P | P | P | P | P | P |
| Commitment of executive management for making IT-related decisions | S | S |  | S | S |  |  |  |  |  |  |  | S |  |  | S |  |  |  |
| IT compliance and support for business compliance with external laws and regulations |  | S |  |  |  | S | S | S |  |  | S | S | P | S | S | P | P |  |  |
| Alignment of IT and business strategy | S | P | S |  | S |  | S |  |  |  |  |  |  | S | S |  | S |  |  |

| | Build, Acquire, and Implement | Deliver, Service and Support | Monitor, Evaluate & Assess |

# Stakeholder needs and enterprise goals

- Table C1 shows how a (non-limitative) list of stakeholder needs can be linked to the enterprise goals.
- Table C2 shows how the same list of stakeholder needs can also be linked to the IT-related goals.

Table C1 Mapping COBIT 5 enterprise goals to typical stakeholder needs

**Enterprise Goals**

| # | Enterprise Goal | How do I know whether I'm compliant with all applicable regulations? | How do I best build and structure my IT department? | What are (control) requirements for information? | Did I address IT-related risk? | Am I running an efficient and resilient IT operation? | How do I control the cost of IT? | How do I know I'm getting value from IT? | Do I have enough people for IT? | How do I develop and maintain skills? | How do I manage (people) performance? | How do I get assurance over IT? |
|---|---|---|---|---|---|---|---|---|---|---|---|---|
| 1 | Compliance with external laws and regulations | ■ | | ■ | ■ | | | | | | | |
| 2 | Managed business risks (safeguarding of assets) | | | ■ | ■ | | | | | | | |
| 3 | Portfolio of competitive products and services | | | | | ■ | | | | | | |
| 4 | Stakeholder value of business investments | | | | | | | ■ | | | | |
| 5 | Financial transparency | | ■ | | | | ■ | | | | | |
| 6 | Customer-oriented service culture | | | | | | | ■ | | | | |
| 7 | Business service continuity and availability | | | | ■ | ■ | | | | | | |
| 8 | Agile responses to a changing business environment | | | | | ■ | | | | ■ | | |
| 9 | Information-based strategic decision making | | | ■ | | | | ■ | | | | |
| 10 | Optimisation of service delivery costs | | ■ | | | ■ | ■ | | | | | |
| 11 | Optimisation of business process functionality | | | ■ | | | | ■ | | | | |
| 12 | Optimisation of business process costs | | | | | | ■ | | | | | |
| 13 | Managed business change programmes | | | | | | | | | | | |
| 14 | Operational and staff productivity | | | | | | | ■ | | | | |
| 15 | Compliance with internal policies | ■ | | | | | | | | | | |
| 16 | Skilled and motivated people | | | | | | | | | ■ | | |
| 17 | Product and business innovation culture | | | | | | | | ■ | | | |

Is the information I am processing well secured?

How do I improve business agility through a more flexible IT environment?

Is it clear what IT is doing?

How often do IT projects fail to deliver what they promised?

How critical is IT to sustaining the enterprise?

How do I know my business partner's operations are secure and reliable?

How do I know the organisation is compliant with applicable rules and regulations?

How do I know the enterprise is maintaining an effective system of internal control?

Table C2 Mapping COBIT 5 IT-related goals to typical stakeholder needs

| IT Goals | | How do I know whether I'm compliant with all applicable regulations? | How do I best build and structure my IT department? | What are (control) requirements for information? | Did I address IT? related risk? | Am I running an efficient and resilient IT operation? | How do I control the cost of IT? | How do I know I'm getting value from IT? | Do I have enough people for IT? |
|---|---|---|---|---|---|---|---|---|---|
| | **Stakeholder Concern** | | | | | | | | |
| 17 | Knowledge, expertise and initiatives for business innovation | | X | | | | | | X |
| 16 | Competent and motivated IT personnel | | | | | | | | X |
| 15 | IT compliance with internal policies | | | | | | X | | X |
| 14 | Availability of reliable and useful information | | | X | | | | | |
| 13 | Delivery of programmes on time, on budget, and meeting requirements and quality standards | | X | | | | | X | |
| 12 | Enablement and support of business processes by integrating applications and technology into business processes | | X | | | | | X | |
| 11 | Optimisation of IT assets, resources, and capabilities | | | | | | X | | |
| 10 | Security of information and processing infrastructure and applications | | | X | | X | | | |
| 9 | IT agility | | X | | | | | | |
| 8 | Adequate use of applications, information, and technology solutions | | | X | | | | | X |
| 7 | Delivery of IT services in line with business requirements | | | | | X | | | |
| 6 | Transparency of IT costs, benefits and risk | | | | | | X | X | |
| 5 | Realised benefits from IT-enabled investments and services portfolio | | | | | | | X | |
| 4 | Managed IT-related business risks | | | | X | | | X | |
| 3 | Commitment of executive management for making IT-related decisions | | X | | | | | | |
| 2 | IT compliance and support for business compliance with external laws and regulations | | X | | | | | | |
| 1 | Alignment of IT and business Strategy | | | | | | | X | |

How do I develop and maintain skills?

How do I manage (people) performance?

How do I get assurance over IT?

Is the information I am processing well secured?

How do I improve business agility through a more flexible IT environment?

Is it clear what IT is doing?

How often do IT projects fail to deliver what they promised?

How critical is IT to sustaining the enterprise?

How do I know my business partner's operations are secure and reliable?

How do I know the organisation is compliant with applicable rules and regulations?

How do I know the enterprise is maintaining an effective system of internal control?

# COBIT 5 vs. COBIT 4.1

How do the seven information criteria of COBIT 4.1 – efficiency, effectiveness, integrity, reliability, availability, confidentiality, reliability – relate to the information quality categories and dimensions of the framework's Information Model (IM)?

This relationship can best be explored through the Product and Service Performance model for Information Quality (PSP/IQ). The PSP/IQ model uses the same quality dimensions as the IM, but organizes them using a different 2 times 2 categorization (on one dimension, product vs. service, and on the other dimension, conforming specifications vs. meeting/exceeding customer expectations) resulting in four information quality categories: soundness, dependability, usefulness, usability:

| | |
|---|---|
| Information as a product | Focus on activities needed to put and maintain data in a database |
| Information as a service | Focus on activities needed to obtain and use information |
| Conforming specifications | Quality perspective that is taken mainly by information producers and custodians |
| Meeting/exceeding customer expectations | Quality perspective that is taken mainly by product/service designers and marketing professionals |

The COBIT information criteria can now be mapped to IM information quality:

- Effectiveness
- Efficiency
- Integrity
- Reliability

- Availability
- Confidentiality
- Compliance

The COBIT 4.1 information criteria are entirely covered by the IM information quality dimension (in the PSP/IQ view) and *vice versa*. Effectiveness is the usefulness category, efficiency is the usability category, and compliance is both the soundness and dependability category. The other COBIT 4.1 information criteria are information quality dimensions within these categories (i.e., reliability is the believability dimension) or are subsumed by information quality dimensions (i.e., integrity, availability and confidentiality are subsumed by, respectively, the free-of-error, accessibility and security dimensions).

# COBIT 5 and ITGI's five governance focus areas

The concepts and ideas contained in these focus areas are maintained and built upon in the framework, but the focus areas themselves have not been literally maintained. Figure E1 provides a brief overview on how the governance aspects in each of the focus areas are covered in the framework.

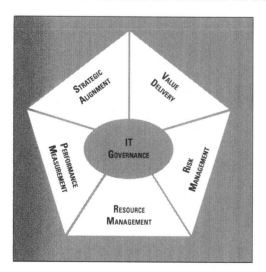

Figure E1  Legacy governance of enterprise IT focus areas

Table E1  Coverage of governance focus areas

| Focus Area | Coverage in COBIT 5 |
|---|---|
| Value Delivery | Covered by the Ensure Value Delivery governance process |
| Risk Management | Covered by the Ensure Risk Management governance process |
| Strategic Alignment | Alignment is not a specific (process) activity, but is achieved through successful execution of the processes in the governance and management areas. The combination of the "evaluate" and "direct" governance practices in the governance area and the resulting direction given to management constitutes alignment. |
| Resource Management | Covered by the Ensure Resource Optimization governance process |
| Performance Measurement | Covered by:<br>• Monitor governance practices in all governance processes<br>• The Report to Stakeholders governance process<br>• By the output(s) from the management processes in the Monitor, Assess and Inform domain |

# Mapping between COBIT 5 and legacy ISACA frameworks

The mapping of COBIT 4.1, Val IT, and Risk IT components to COBIT 5 is shown in Tables F1, F2, and F3.

## COBIT 4.1

Table F1  COBIT 4.1 control objectives mapped to COBIT 5

| COBIT 4.1 – Control Objectives | | Covered in COBIT 5 by: |
|---|---|---|
| PO1.1 | IT value management assumes all these titles have been checked against CobiT? | EDM2 |
| PO1.2 | Business-IT alignment | APO2.1 |
| PO1.3 | Assessment of current capability and performance | APO2.2 |
| PO1.4 | IT strategic plan | APO2.3-5 |
| PO1.5 | Tactical IT plans | APO2.5 |
| PO1.6 | IT portfolio management | APO5.5 |
| PO2.1 | Enterprise information architecture model | APO3.2 |
| PO2.2 | Enterprise data dictionary and data syntax rules | APO3.2 |
| PO2.3 | Data classification scheme | APO3.2 |
| PO2.4 | Integrity management | APO1.6 |
| PO3.1 | Technological direction planning | APO2.3, APO4.3 |
| PO3.2 | Technical infrastructure plan | APO2.3-5, APO4.3-5 |
| PO3.3 | Monitor future trends and regulations | EDM1.1, APO4.2 |
| PO3.4 | Technology standards | APO3.5 |
| PO3.5 | IT architecture board | APO1.1 |
| PO4.1 | IT process framework | APO1.3, APO1.7 |

| COBIT 4.1 – Control Objectives | | Covered in COBIT 5 by: |
|---|---|---|
| PO4.2 | IT strategy committee | APO1.1 |
| PO4.3 | IT steering committee | APO1.1 |
| PO4.4 | Organizational placement of the IT function | APO1.5 |
| PO4.5 | It organizational structure | APO1.1 |
| PO4.6 | Establishment of roles and responsibilities | APO1.2 |
| PO4.7 | Responsibility for IT quality assurance | APO11.1 |
| PO4.8 | Responsibility for risk, security and compliance *DELETED* These specific roles are no longer explicitly specified as a practice | |
| PO4.9 | Data, and system ownership | APO1.6 |
| PO4.10 | Supervision | APO1.2 |
| PO4.11 | Segregation of duties | DSS7.4, DSS8.2 |
| PO4.12 | IT staffing | APO7.1 |
| PO4.13 | Key IT personnel | APO7.2 |
| PO4.14 | Contracted staff policies, and procedures | APO7.6 |
| PO4.15 | Relationships | APO1.1 |
| PO5.1 | Financial management framework | APO6.1 |
| PO5.2 | Prioritization within IT budget | APO6.2 |
| PO5.3 | IT budgeting | APO6.3 |
| PO5.4 | Cost management | APO6.4, APO6.5 |
| PO5.5 | Benefit management | APO5.6 |
| PO6.1 | IT policy and control environment | APO1.3 |
| PO6.2 | Enterprise IT risk and control framework | EDM3.2 |
| PO6.3 | IT policies management | APO1.3, APO1.8 |
| PO6.4 | Policy, standard and procedures rollout | APO1.3, APO1.8 |
| PO6.5 | Communication of IT objectives and direction | APO7.6 |
| PO7.1 | Personnel recruitment and retention | APO7.1 |
| PO7.2 | Personnel competencies | APO7.3 |
| PO7.3 | Staffing of roles | APO1.2, APO7.1 |
| PO7.4 | Personnel training | APO7.3 |
| PO7.5 | Dependence upon individuals | APO7.2 |
| PO7.6 | Personnel clearance procedures | APO7.1 |
| PO7.7 | Employee job performance evaluation | APO7.4 |
| PO7.8 | Job change and termination | APO7.1 |
| PO8.1 | Quality management system | APO11.1 |
| PO8.2 | IT standards and quality practices | APO11.2 |
| PO8.3 | Development and acquisition standards | APO11.2, APO11.5 |
| PO8.4 | Customer focus | APO11.3 |
| PO8.5 | Continuous improvement | APO11.6 |
| PO8.6 | Quality measurement, monitoring and review | APO11.4 |
| PO9.1 | IT risk management framework | EDM03.2 |
| PO9.2 | Establishment of risk context | APO12.3 |
| PO9.3 | Event identification | APO12.1, APO12.3 |

| COBIT 4.1 – Control Objectives | | Covered in COBIT 5 by: |
|---|---|---|
| PO9.4 | Risk assessment | APO12.2, APO12.4 |
| PO9.5 | Risk response | APO12.6 |
| PO9.6 | Maintenance and monitoring of a risk action plan | APO12.4, APO12.5 |
| PO10.1 | Program management framework | BAI1.1 |
| PO10.2 | Project management framework | BAI1.1 |
| PO10.3 | Project management approach | BAI1.1 |
| PO10.4 | Stakeholder commitment | BAI1.3 |
| PO10.5 | Project scope statement | BAI1.7 |
| PO10.6 | Project phase initiation | BAI1.7 |
| PO10.7 | Integrated project plan | BAI1.8 |
| PO10.8 | Project resources | BAI1.8 |
| PO10.9 | Project risk management | BAI1.10 |
| PO10.10 | Project quality plan | BAI1.9 |
| PO10.11 | Project change control | BAI1.11 |
| PO10.12 | Project planning of assurance methods | BAI1.8 |
| PO10.13 | Project performance measurement, reporting, and monitoring | BAI1.6, BAI1.11 |
| PO10.14 | Project closure | BAI1.13 |
| AI1.1 | Definition and maintenance of business functional and technical requirements | BAI2.1 |
| AI1.2 | Risk analysis report | BAI2.3 |
| AI1.3 | Feasibility study and formulation of alternative courses of action | BAI2.2 |
| AI1.4 | Requirements and feasibility decision and approval | BAI2.4 |
| AI2.1 | High-level design | BAI3.1 |
| AI2.2 | Detailed design | BAI3.2 |
| AI2.3 | Application control and auditability | BAI3.5 |
| AI2.4 | Application security and availability | BAI3.1, BAI3.2, BAI3.3, BAI3.5 |
| AI2.5 | Configuration and implementation of acquired application software | BAI3.3, BAI3.5 |
| AI2.6 | Major upgrades to existing systems | BAI3.10 |
| AI2.7 | Development of application software | BAI3.3, BAI3.4 |
| AI2.8 | Software quality assurance | BAI3.6 |
| AI2.9 | Applications requirements management | BAI3.9 |
| AI2.10 | Application software maintenance | BAI3.10 |
| AI3.1 | Technological infrastructure acquisition plan | BAI3.4 |
| AI3.2 | Infrastructure resource protection, and availability | BAI3.3 |
| AI3.3 | Infrastructure maintenance | BAI3.10 |
| AI3.4 | Feasibility test environment | BAI3.7, BAI3.8 |
| AI4.1 | Planning for operational solutions | BAI5.5 |
| AI4.2 | Knowledge transfer to business management | BAI8.1, BAI8.2, BAI8.3, BAI8.4 |
| AI4.3 | Knowledge transfer to end users | BAI8.1, BAI8.2, BAI8.3, BAI8.4 |

| COBIT 4.1 – Control Objectives | | Covered in COBIT 5 by: |
|---|---|---|
| AI4.4 | Knowledge transfer to operations and support staff | BAI8.1, BAI8.2, BAI8.3, BAI8.4 |
| AI5.1 | Procurement control | BAI3.4 |
| AI5.2 | Supplier contract management | APO10.1, APO10.3 |
| AI5.3 | Supplier selection | APO10.2 |
| AI5.4 | IT resources acquisition | APO10.3 |
| AI6.1 | Change standards and procedures | BAI6.1, BAI6.2, BAI6.3, BAI6.4 |
| AI6.2 | Impact assessment, prioritization and authorization | BAI6.1 |
| AI6.3 | Emergency changes | BAI6.2 |
| AI6.4 | Change status tracking and reporting | BAI6.3 |
| AI6.5 | Change closure and documentation | BAI6.4 |
| AI7.1 | Training | BAI5.5 |
| AI7.2 | Test plan | BAI7.1, BAI7.3 |
| AI7.3 | Implementation plan | BAI7.1 |
| AI7.4 | Test environment | BAI7.4 |
| AI7.5 | System and data conversion | BAI7.2 |
| AI7.6 | Testing of changes | BAI7.5 |
| AI7.7 | Final acceptance test | BAI7.5 |
| AI7.8 | Promotion to production | BAI7.6 |
| AI7.9 | Post-implementation review | BAI7.8 |
| DS1.1 | Service level management framework | APO9.1, APO9.2, APO9.3, APO9.4, APO9.5, APO9.6 |
| DS1.2 | Definition of services | APO9.1, APO9.2, APO9.3 |
| DS1.3 | Service level agreements | APO9.4 |
| DS1.4 | Operating level agreements | APO9.4 |
| DS1.5 | Monitoring and reporting of service level achievements | APO9.5 |
| DS1.6 | Review of service level agreements and contracts | APO9.6 |
| DS2.1 | Identification of all supplier relationships | APO10.1 |
| DS2.2 | Supplier relationship management | APO10.3 |
| DS2.3 | Supplier risk management | APO10.4 |
| DS2.4 | Supplier performance monitoring | APO10.5 |
| DS3.1 | Performance and capacity planning | BAI4.3 |
| DS3.2 | Current performance and capacity | BAI4.1, BAI4.2 |
| DS3.3 | Future performance, and capacity | BAI4.1 |
| DS3.4 | IT resources availability | BAI4.5 |
| DS3.5 | Monitoring and reporting | BAI4.4 |
| DS4.1 | IT continuity framework | DSS6.1, DSS6.2 |
| DS4.2 | IT continuity plans | DSS6.3 |
| DS4.3 | Critical IT resources | DSS6.4 |
| DS4.4 | Maintenance of the IT continuity plan | DSS6.2, DSS6.6 |
| DS4.5 | Testing of the IT continuity plan | DSS6.5 |

| COBIT 4.1 – Control Objectives | | Covered in COBIT 5 by: |
|---|---|---|
| DS4.6 | IT continuity plan training | DSS6.7 |
| DS4.7 | Distribution of the IT continuity plan | DSS6.3 |
| DS4.8 | IT services recovery and resumption | DSS6.4 |
| DS4.9 | Offsite backup storage | DSS6.8 |
| DS4.10 | Post-resumption review | DSS6.9 |
| DS5.1 | Management of IT security | DSS7.1 |
| DS5.2 | IT security plan | APO1.6 |
| DS5.3 | Identity management | DSS7.4 |
| DS5.4 | User account management | DSS7.4 |
| DS5.5 | Security testing surveillance, and monitoring | DSS7.2 |
| DS5.6 | Security incident definition | DSS7.7 |
| DS5.7 | Protection of security technology | DSS7.6 |
| DS5.8 | Cryptographic key management | DSS7.8 |
| DS5.9 | Malicious software prevention, detection and correction | DSS7.1 |
| DS5.10 | Network security | DSS7.2 |
| DS5.11 | Exchange of sensitive data | DSS7.2 |
| DS6.1 | Definition of services | APO6.4 |
| DS6.2 | IT accounting | APO6.1 |
| DS6.3 | Cost modeling and charging | APO6.4 |
| DS6.4 | Cost model maintenance | APO6.4 |
| DS7.1 | Identification of education and training needs | APO7.3 |
| DS7.2 | Delivery of training and education | APO7.3 |
| DS7.3 | Evaluation of training received | APO7.3 |
| DS8.1 | Service desk<br>*DELETED*<br>ITIL 3 does not refer to service desk as a process | |
| DS8.2 | Registration of customer queries | DSS4.1, DSS4.2, DSS4.3 |
| DS8.3 | Incident escalation | DSS4.4 |
| DS8.4 | Incident closure | DSS4.5, DSS4.6 |
| DS8.5 | Reporting and trend analysis | DSS4.7 |
| DS9.1 | Configuration repository and baseline | DSS3.1, DSS3.2, DSS3.4 |
| DS9.2 | Identification and maintenance of configuration items | DSS3.3 |
| DS9.3 | Configuration integrity review | DSS3.4, DSS3.5 |
| DS10.1 | Identification and classification of problems | DSS5.1 |
| DS10.2 | Problem tracking and resolution | DSS5.2 |
| DS10.3 | Problem closure | DSS5.3, DSS5.4 |
| DS10.4 | Integration of configuration, incident, and problem management | DSS5.5 |
| DS11.1 | Business requirements for data management | DSS1.1 |
| DS11.2 | Storage, and retention arrangements | DSS6.8, DSS8.4 |
| DS11.3 | Media library management system | DSS6.8 |
| DS11.4 | Disposal | DSS7.8 |
| DS11.5 | Backup and restoration | DSS6.8 |

| COBIT 4.1 – Control Objectives | | Covered in COBIT 5 by: |
|---|---|---|
| DS11.6 | Security requirements for data management | DSS1.1, DSS7.8, DSS8.5 |
| DS12.1 | Site selection and layout | DSS7.5 |
| DS12.2 | Physical security measures | DSS7.5 |
| DS12.3 | Physical access | DSS7.5 |
| DS12.4 | Protection against environmental factors | DSS1.4 |
| DS12.5 | Physical facilities management | DSS1.5 |
| DS13.1 | Operations procedures and instructions | DSS1.1 |
| DS13.2 | Job scheduling | DSS1.1 |
| DS13.3 | IT infrastructure monitoring | DSS1.3 |
| DS13.4 | Sensitive documents and output devices | DSS7.6 |
| DS13.5 | Preventive maintenance for hardware | DSS2.2 |
| ME1.1 | Monitoring approach | MEA1.1 |
| ME1.2 | Definition and collection of monitoring data | MEA1.2, MEA1.3 |
| ME1.3 | Monitoring method | MEA1.3 |
| ME1.4 | Performance assessment | MEA1.4 |
| ME1.5 | Board and executive reporting | MEA1.4 |
| ME1.6 | Remedial actions | MEA1.5 |
| ME2.1 | Monitoring of internal control framework | MEA2.1, MEA2.2 |
| ME2.2 | Supervisory review | MEA2.1 |
| ME2.3 | Control exceptions | MEA2.4 |
| ME2.4 | Control self-assessment | MEA2.3 |
| ME2.5 | Assurance of internal control | MEA2.6, MEA2.7, MEA2.8 |
| ME2.6 | Internal control at third parties | MEA2.1 |
| ME2.7 | Remedial actions | MEA2.4 |
| ME3.1 | Identification of external legal, regulatory and contractual compliance requirements | MEA3.1 |
| ME3.2 | Optimization of response to external requirements | MEA3.2 |
| ME3.3 | Evaluation of compliance with external requirements | MEA3.3 |
| ME3.4 | Positive assurance of compliance | MEA3.4 |
| ME3.5 | Integrated reporting | MEA3.4 |
| ME4.1 | Establishment of a framework for governance of enterprise IT | EDM1 |
| ME4.2 | Strategic alignment _DELETED_ Alignment is now considered to be the result of all governance and management activities | |
| ME4.3 | Value delivery | EDM2 |
| ME4.4 | Resource management | EDM4 |
| ME4.5 | Risk management | EDM3 |
| ME4.6 | Performance measurement | EDM1.3, EDM2.3, EDM3.3, EDM4.3 |
| ME4.7 | Independent assurance | EDM2.5, EDM2.6, EDM2.7, EDM2.8 |

# Val IT

Table F2 Val IT 2.0 key management practices covered by COBIT 5

| Val IT 2.0 Key Management Practices | | Covered in COBIT 5 by: |
|---|---|---|
| VG1.1 | Develop an understanding of the significance of IT and the role of governance | EDM1.1 |
| VG1.2 | Establish effective reporting lines | EDM1.1 |
| VG1.3 | Establish a leadership forum | EDM1.2, AP01.1 |
| VG1.4 | Define value for the enterprise | EDM2.2 |
| VG1.5 | Ensure alignment, and integration of business and IT strategies with key business goals | AP02.1 |
| VG2.1 | Define the value governance framework | EDM1.2 |
| VG2.2 | Assess the quality and coverage of current processes | AP01.7 |
| VG2.3 | Identify and prioritize process requirements | AP01.7 |
| VG2.4 | Define and document the processes | AP01.7 |
| VG2.5 | Establish, implement and communicate roles, responsibilities, and accountabilities | AP01.2 |
| VG2.6 | Establish organizational structures | EDM1.2, AP01.2 |
| VG3.1 | Define portfolio types | EDM2.2 |
| VG3.2 | Define categories (within portfolios) | EDM2.2 |
| VG3.3 | Develop and communicate evaluation criteria (for each category) | EDM2.2 |
| VG3.4 | Assign weightings to criteria | EDM2.2 |
| VG3.5 | Define requirements for stage-gates, and other reviews (for each category) | EDM2.2 |
| VG4.1 | Review current enterprise budgeting practices | AP06.3 |
| VG4.2 | Determine value management financial planning practice requirements | AP06.1 |
| VG4.3 | Identify changes required | AP06.1 |
| VG4.4 | Implement optimal financial planning practices for value management | AP06.1 |
| VG5.1 | Identify key metrics | EDM2.3 |
| VG5.2 | Define information capture processes, and approaches | EDM2.3 |
| VG5.3 | Define reporting methods and techniques | EDM2.3 |
| VG5.4 | Identify and monitor performance improvement actions | EDM2.3 |
| VG6.1 | Implement lessons learned | EDM2.3 |
| PM1.1 | Review and ensure clarity of the business strategy, and goals | AP05.1 |
| PM1.2 | Identify opportunities for IT to influence, and support the business strategy | AP05.1 |
| PM1.3 | Define an appropriate investment mix | AP05.1 |
| PM1.4 | Translate the business strategy and goals into IT strategy and goals | AP05.1 |
| PM2.1 | Determine overall investment funds | AP05.2 |
| PM3.1 | Create and maintain an inventory of business human resources | AP07.1 |

| Val IT 2.0 Key Management Practices | | Covered in COBIT 5 by: |
|---|---|---|
| PM3.2 | Understand the current and future demand (for business human resources) | APO7.1 |
| PM3.2 | Identify shortfalls (between current and future business human resource demand) | APO7.1 |
| PM3.4 | Create and maintain tactical plans (for business human resources) | APO7.1 |
| PM3.5 | Monitor, review and adjust (business function allocation and staffing) | APO7.5 |
| PM3.6 | Create and maintain an inventory of IT human resources | APO7.5 |
| PM3.7 | Understand the current and future demand (for IT human resources) | APO7.5 |
| PM3.8 | Identify shortfalls (between current and future IT human resource demand) | APO7.5 |
| PM3.9 | Create and maintain tactical plans (for IT human resources) | APO7.5 |
| PM3.10 | Monitor, review and adjust (IT function allocation and staffing) | APO7.5 |
| PM4.1 | Evaluate and assign relative scores to program business cases | APO5.3 |
| PM4.2 | Create an overall investment portfolio view | APO5.3 |
| PM4.3 | Make and communicate investment decisions | APO5.3 |
| PM4.4 | Specify stage-gates and allocate funds to selected programs | APO5.3 |
| PM4.5 | Adjust business targets, forecasts, and budgets | APO5.3 |
| PM5.1 | Monitor and report on investment portfolio performance | APO5.4 |
| PM6.1 | Optimize investment portfolio performance | APO5.4 |
| PM6.2 | Reprioritize the investment portfolio | APO5.4 |
| IM1.1 | Recognize investment opportunities | APO5.3 |
| IM1.2 | Develop the initial program concept business case | BAI1.2 |
| IM1.3 | Evaluate the initial program concept business case | APO5.3 |
| IM2.1 | Develop a clear and complete understanding of the candidate program | BAI1.2 |
| IM2.2 | Perform analysis of the alternatives | BAI1.2 |
| IM3.1 | Develop the program plan | BAI1.4 |
| IM4.1 | Identify full lifecycle costs, and benefits | BAI1.4 |
| IM4.2 | Develop a benefits realization plan | BAI1.4 |
| IM4.3 | Perform appropriate reviews, and obtain sign-offs | BAI1.3, BAI1.4 |
| IM5.1 | Develop the detailed program business case | BAI1.2 |
| IM5.2 | Assign clear accountability and ownership | BAI1.2 |
| IM5.3 | Perform appropriate reviews and obtain sign-offs | BAI1.2, BAI1.3 |
| IM6.1 | Plan projects, and resource, and launch the program | BAI1.5 |
| IM6.2 | Manage the program | BAI1.5 |
| IM6.3 | Track and manage benefits | BAI1.5 |
| IM7.1 | Update operational IT portfolios | APO5.5 |
| IM8.1 | Update the business case | BAI1.4 |
| IM9.1 | Monitor and report on program (solution delivery) performance | BAI1.6 |
| IM9.2 | Monitor and report on business (benefit/outcome) performance | BAI1.6 |

| Val IT 2.0 Key Management Practices | | Covered in COBIT 5 by: |
|---|---|---|
| IM9.3 | Monitor and report on operational (service delivery) performance | BAI1.6 |
| IM10.1 | Retire the program | BAI1.14 |

# Risk IT

Table F3  Risk IT key management practices covered by COBIT 5

| Risk IT Key Management Practices | | Covered in COBIT 5 by: |
|---|---|---|
| RG1.1 | Perform enterprise IT risk assessment | EDM3.1, APO12.2-3 |
| RG1.2 | Propose IT risk tolerance thresholds | EDM3.1 |
| RG1.3 | Approve IT risk tolerance | EDM3.1, EDM3.2 |
| RG1.4 | Align IT risk policy | EDM3.1, EDM3.2 |
| RG1.5 | Promote IT risk-aware culture | EDM3.2 |
| RG1.6 | Encourage effective communication of IT risk | EDM3.3 |
| RG2.1 | Establish and maintain accountability for IT Risk Management | EDM3.2 |
| RG2.2 | Co-ordinate IT risk strategy, and business risk strategy | EDM3.1, EDM3.2 |
| RG2.3 | Adapt IT risk practices to enterprise risk practices | EDM3.1, EDM3.2 |
| RG2.4 | Provide adequate resources for IT risk management | EDM4.1, APO7.1, APO7.3 |
| RG2.5 | Gain management buy-in for the IT risk analysis approach | EDM1.1-2, EDM3.2 |
| RG3.2 | Approve IT risk analysis | EDM3.1 |
| RG3.3 | Embed IT risk considerations in strategic business decision making | EDM3.1 |
| RG3.4 | Accept IT risk | EDM3.1 |
| RG3.5 | Prioritize it risk response activities | EDM3.2 |
| RE1.1 | Establish and maintain a model for data collection | APO12.1 |
| RE1.2 | Collect data on the operating environment | APO12.1 |
| RE1.3 | Collect data on risk events | APO12.1 |
| RE1.4 | Identify risk factors | APO12.1 |
| RE2.1 | Define IT risk analysis scope | APO12.2 |
| RE2.2 | Estimate IT risk | APO12.2 |
| RE2.3 | Identify risk response options | APO12.2 |
| RE2.4 | Perform a peer review of IT risk analysis | APO12.2 |
| RE3.1 | Map IT resources to business processes | APO12.2 |
| RE3.2 | Determine business criticality of IT resources | APO12.3 |
| RE3.3 | Understand IT capabilities | APO12.3 |
| RE3.4 | Update IT risk scenario components | APO12.3 |
| RE3.5 | Maintain the IT risk register and IT risk map | APO12.3 |
| RE3.6 | Develop IT risk indicators | APO12.3 |
| RR1.1 | Communicate IT risk analysis results | APO12.4 |
| RR1.2 | Report IT risk management activities and state of compliance | APO12.4 |

| Risk IT Key Management Practices | | Covered in COBIT 5 by: |
|---|---|---|
| RR1.3 | Interpret independent IT assessment findings | APO12.4 |
| RR 1.4 | Identify IT-related opportunities | APO12.4 |
| RR2.1 | Inventory controls | APO12.5 |
| RR2.2 | Monitor operational alignment with risk tolerance thresholds | APO12.5 |
| RR2.3 | Respond to discovered risk exposure, and opportunity | APO12.5 |
| RR2.4 | Implement controls | APO12.5 |
| RR2.5 | Report IT risk action plan progress | APO12.5 |
| RR3.1 | Maintain incident response plans | APO12.6 |
| RR3.2 | Monitor IT risk | APO12.6 |
| RR3.3 | Initiate incident response | APO12.6 |
| RR3.4 | Communicate lessons learned from risk events | APO12.6 |

# About ISACA®

ISACA is the single international source for information technology controls. ISACA helps its members and their employers ensure trust in, and value from, information systems.

## History and Mission

A nonprofit, independent membership association, ISACA is a leading global provider of knowledge, certifications, community, advocacy, and education on information systems assurance, control, and security, enterprise governance of IT, and IT-related risk and compliance. Founded in 1969 as the EDP Auditors Association, ISACA helps its members and their employers ensure trust in, and value from, information systems.

## Membership

ISACA—formerly the Information Systems Audit and Control Association—has more than 100,000 constituents in more than 180 countries in Asia, Latin America, Europe, Africa, North America and Oceania. Its members include internal and external auditors, CEOs, CFOs, CIOs, educators, information security and control professionals, business managers, students, and IT consultants.

With 95,000 constituents in 160 countries, ISACA (*www.isaca.org*) is a leading global provider of knowledge, certifications, community, advocacy, and education on information systems (IS) assurance and security, organizational governance and management of IT, and IT-related risk and compliance. Founded in 1969, the non-profit, independent ISACA hosts international conferences, publishes the

*ISACA® Journal*, and develops international IS auditing and control standards, which help its constituents ensure trust in, and value from, information systems. ISACA also advances and attests IT skills and knowledge through the globally respected Certified Information Systems Auditor® (CISA®), Certified Information Security Manager® (CISM®), Certified in the Governance of Enterprise IT® (CGEIT®) and Certified in Risk and Information Systems Control™ (CRISC™) designations. ISACA continually updates COBIT®, which helps IT professionals and enterprise leaders fulfill their governance of enterprise IT and management responsibilities, particularly in the areas of assurance, security, risk, and control, and deliver value to the business.

## Disclaimer

This publication is based on ISACA's *COBIT® 5: The Framework* (the "Work"). The author of this management guide, Van Haren Publishing and ISACA make no claim that using either publication will assure a successful outcome. The publications should not be considered inclusive of all proper information, procedures, and tests or exclusive of other information, procedures, and tests that are reasonably directed to obtaining the same results. Readers should use their own professional judgment based on their enterprise's unique circumstances.

## Reservation of Rights of ISACA material

ISACA
3701 Algonquin Road, Suite 1010
Rolling Meadows, IL 60008 USA
Phone: +1.847.253.1545
Fax: +1.847.253.1443
E-mail: *info@isaca.org*
Web site: *www.isaca.org*

COBIT is a trademark/service mark of ISACA. The mark has been applied for or
registered in countries throughout the world.